Expert Oracle Application Express Plug-Ins

Building Reusable Components

Martin Giffy D'Souza

Apress®

Expert Oracle Application Express Plug-Ins: Building Reusable Components

Copyright © 2011 by Martin Giffy D'Souza

ISBN-13 (pbk): 978-1-4302-3503-3

ISBN-13 (electronic): 978-1-4302-3504-0

President and Publisher: Paul Manning
Lead Editor: Jonathan Gennick
Technical Reviewer: Edmund Zehoo
Editorial Board: Steve Anglin, Mark Beckner, Ewan Buckingham, Gary Cornell, Morgan Ertel, Jonathan Gennick, Jonathan Hassell, Robert Hutchinson, Michelle Lowman, James Markham, Matthew Moodie, Jeff Olson, Jeffrey Pepper, Douglas Pundick, Ben Renow-Clarke, Dominic Shakeshaft, Gwenan Spearing, Matt Wade, Tom Welsh
Coordinating Editor: Adam Heath
Copy Editor: Mary Ann Fugate
Compositor: Apress Production (Christine Ricketts)
Indexer: SPI Global
Artist: SPI Global
Cover Designer: Anna Ishchenko

Distributed to the book trade worldwide by Springer Science+Business Media, NY., 233 Spring Street, 6th Floor, New York, NY 10013. Phone 1-800-SPRINGER, fax (201) 348-4505, e-mail orders-ny@springer-sbm.com, or visit www.springeronline.com.

For information on translations, please e-mail rights@apress.com, or visit www.apress.com.

Apress and friends of ED books may be purchased in bulk for academic, corporate, or promotional use. eBook versions and licenses are also available for most titles. For more information, reference our Special Bulk Sales–eBook Licensing web page at www.apress.com/bulk-sales.

Any source code or other supplementary materials referenced by the author in this text is available to readers at www.apress.com. For detailed information about how to locate your book's source code, go to http://www.apress.com/source-code/.

Contents at a Glance

Contents

About the Author

Martin Giffy D'Souza is a co-founder and CTO at ClariFit Inc. (www.clarifit.com), a consulting firm and custom solutions provider that specializes in APEX and PL/SQL development. Martin's experience in the technology industry has been focused on developing database-centric web applications using the Oracle APEX technology stack.

Prior to co-founding ClariFit Inc., Martin's career has seen him hold a range of positions within award-winning companies. Martin is also the author of the highly recognized blog, www.TalkApex.com, which boasts a multitude of posts on a wide array of APEX-focused topics. He has also presented at numerous international conferences such as APEXposed, COUG, and ODTUG, for which he won the Presenter of the Year award in 2011.

Martin is an Oracle ACE and holds a computer engineering degree from Queen's University in Kingston, Ontario, Canada.

About the Technical Reviewer

Edmund T. Zehoo is the chief technology officer and co-founder of Arigoo Pte Ltd., an e-forms and workflows solution vendor based in Singapore. He was the lead architect in the four-year design of Arigoo's flagship product from scratch, which is now a mature product in Singapore with a list of multinational corporate customers to its name. He also holds more than eight years of experience in building performance-critical .NET e-forms and workflows solutions hosted on top of Oracle databases for large companies and governmental institutions located in Singapore

Acknowledgments

This book wouldn't have been possible if it weren't for several individuals who have helped out behind the scenes, providing support through answering questions and giving me some ideas and feedback. More specifically, thanks to Patrick Wolf and Daniel McGhan for their input and excellent recommendations. As well thanks to my business partners, Cameron Mahbubian and Chris Hritzuk, for working extra hard on the business to allow me to focus on this book.

Of course, it goes without saying that I'd like to thank my family. Despite the fact that they have no idea what a database is (in spite of my many attempts to try to explain it to them), they've always been very supportive of everything I do and this book was no different. Thanks to my parents, Norbert and Susanne, for all their support and guidance.

There's a saying that goes, "Behind every great man, there's an even greater woman." Special thanks to my partner, Stephanie Schubert, for being understanding and supportive over some very late nights as I wrote this book. Without her support, this book wouldn't have happened.

—Martin Giffy D'Souza

Introduction

When APEX 4.0 was first released, I was very excited about all of the new features and fixes. The two new features that interested me the most were dynamic actions and plug-ins. I was fortunate to be able to write about dynamic actions in the *Expert Oracle Application Express* book earlier this year. When the opportunity presented itself to write a book entirely dedicated to plug-ins, I couldn't resist.

After writing countless examples on how to modify APEX on my blog, `www.talkapex.com`, I was ecstatic when plug-ins were introduced to APEX. They offer developers a standardized, declarative way to write customized objects in APEX and easily reuse them within an application. Of course, you can share plug-ins with your organization or even with the entire APEX community. I've written many free plug-ins, which can be found at `plugins.clarifit.com` and are available for download at `www.apex-plugin.com`.

Halfway through writing this book, APEX 4.1 was released. APEX 4.1 introduced some new features and enhancements to the plug-in framework, and I decided to go back and re-write several sections in this book to reflect the changes between versions. The only thing from the new plug-in features introduced in APEX 4.1 that is not covered in this book is the two new types of plug-ins: authorization and authentication. The four other types of plug-ins are covered in detail in this book, and you should be able to leverage the knowledge obtained from them to help yourself write authorization and authentication plug-ins.

This book provides you with all the necessary information to get a solid foundation of how to build an APEX plug-in. It also includes information on some tools that will be helpful to you when developing plug-ins. You may find it helpful to flip back and forth between your current page and Chapters 7 and 8, which focus on best practices, debugging, and tools.

Once you finish this book, or even get through the first example plug-in, I encourage you to try to create your own plug-in. It will feel awkward at first, and you will inevitably run into some issues on your first try. Don't get discouraged and stop. With some extra work, you will get the knack of how plug-ins work and will learn to love writing them soon enough. Once you get the hang of them, you will never go back.

My best advice for writing your first plug-in is to choose a really simple problem and go from there. The first time I took a stab at writing a plug-in, I had a complex issue I was trying to solve. After many hours, I had to scrap all my work and start over with the goal of solving a simple problem first. Throughout the book, I emphasize always listing out your requirements before writing a single line of code. I hope you follow this advice, which will inevitably save you time.

Good luck, and I hope you enjoy this book and find it helpful.

—Martin Giffy D'Souza

CHAPTER 1

■ ■ ■

Introduction to Plug-Ins

Plug-ins allow third-party developers to add additional functionality to software applications and frameworks. Plug-ins exist for many different types of applications, such Mozilla Firefox (Add-ons and Extensions), Microsoft Word (Add-Ins), and development frameworks such as Salesforce.com.

As Oracle Application Express (APEX) has been growing, so have the requests from the APEX community for specific features. To the best of their ability, the team from Oracle that develops APEX has modified the product to meet these demands; however, it's not fair to assume that they can add in every request that they receive. For this reason, the plug-ins framework was created. Starting in APEX 4.0, the APEX framework was extended to allow all developers to create their own plug-ins to add additional functionality in a supported and declarative way. APEX plug-ins can be shared within organizations and with the entire APEX community.

About This Book

This book provides step-by-step instructions on how to build plug-ins, along with detailed explanations about all the available options for plug-ins. It also contains some useful tools, techniques, and best practices to help ensure successful plug-in development and implementation. This book is targeted toward intermediate to advanced-level APEX developers.

It is assumed that you know the fundamentals of APEX and have developed some applications with it. If you are new to APEX, you're encouraged to read a beginners book and then use this one to further enhance your APEX development skill set. A recommended book for new developers is *Beginning Oracle Application Express 4*, which is also published by Apress.

Besides basic knowledge about APEX, this book assumes you are comfortable with the languages and frameworks listed here. If you need to brush up on some of the web-based technologies, www.w3schools.com has some excellent free tutorials to help you learn.

- PL/SQL

- JavaScript (JS)

- jQuery

- CSS

- HTML

1

■ **Note** This book contains examples on how to build all the different types of plug-ins. All the plug-ins that are highlighted in this book are open source plug-ins that can be easily integrated into commercial applications without concern about licensing.

Plug-Ins and Their Advantages

Plug-ins allow APEX developers to create their own supported and declarative objects in APEX. When developed correctly, plug-ins behave exactly like native APEX objects and are seamless for both developers and users alike.

There are several types of plug-ins that can currently be developed. Some of them focus on the user interface (UI), and some are for process only. Page process plug-ins can go either way, because you can use them during rendering to manipulate what the user sees, *and* during page processing to perform back-end work. Most often, process plug-ins are used for back-end processing.

Following are the plug-in types available:

- UI / Front-end related
    - Dynamic action
    - Item
    - Region
- Process / Back-end related
    - Authorization *
    - Authentication *
    - Process

■ **Note** Plug-ins tagged with a " *" are new to 4.1. Since they are extremely new to APEX (at the time of writing), they will not be covered in this book.

As APEX evolved, developers started to create their own frameworks to integrate new and advanced features in APEX. These custom frameworks made it difficult to manage and maintain applications. Plug-ins resolve the need for custom frameworks as they provide a declarative way to develop custom objects within APEX.

Besides removing the need for customized frameworks, plug-ins allow developers to easily share plug-ins within an organization and the community. Previously, when developers integrated a new feature in APEX, they would share it via a blog post. Other developers would need to copy and then modify the code to merge it into their application. If third-party files, such as JavaScript or CSS files, were required, you would need to integrate them into your application somehow. All these moving parts made it complex to share ideas and code. Plug-ins encapsulate all that complexity and remove the dependencies, since they bundle all the required objects into a single item, which can be easily shared.

Getting Started

*WAIT!*You are probably eager to start learning to develop your first plug-in, but don't skip over this section. The rest of the book assumes that you have all the necessary tools in place to successfully and efficiently develop plug-ins. This section will cover all the tools you'll need throughout this book.

Oracle Database

Before using APEX, you'll need to have an Oracle database to develop on. All the examples in this book were built on an Oracle 11gR2 instance. Some of the code may not be compatible with previous versions of Oracle but can be easily modified to work with older versions.

There are several options to choose from depending on your current situation. If you have access to a development instance of Oracle 11gR2, then you can skip this subsection. If not, there are several easy options for you:

> apex.oracle.com: Oracle provides a free online instance of APEX for development purposes. The SQL Workshop will allow you to create and modify PL/SQL code. This is the easiest solution to setup; however, it will be cumbersome to develop and debug PL/SQL code via a web interface. You may encounter some restrictions connecting to external resources (such as web services) using apex.oracle.com for the examples in this book.

> *Oracle XE*: Oracle provides a free (both for commercial and personal use) database called Oracle XE. It is an ideal option for installing a personal instance of Oracle. Oracle XE does have some size and functional limitations, but they should not hinder your ability to build plug-ins or follow the examples in this book. For more information about how to download and install Oracle XE, go to the following OTN page:
> www.oracle.com/technetwork/database/express-edition/overview/index.html.

> *Virtual machine*: Oracle provides a virtual machine image thatis a full version of 11gR2. You'll first need to install Oracle Virtual Box:
> www.oracle.com/technetwork/server-storage/virtualbox/index.html. The developer virtual machine image can be downloaded from the OTN Developer Days page:
> www.oracle.com/technetwork/database/enterprise-edition/databaseappdev-vm-161299.html.

> *Install Oracle*: If you want a full version of Oracle directly, you can obtain a developer's license and download a copy from OTN:
> www.oracle.com/technetwork/database/enterprise-edition/overview/index.html. This is not a recommended approach for non-DBAs as it can take a while to properly configure Oracle from scratch.Of the four options just listed, Oracle XE may be the best option to implement on a personal or work PC. Each of the links provides installation instructions where applicable. Before installing or using any of the foregoingoptions, please read the licensing agreements.

APEX Instance

If you're using a corporate database or a personal instance, you'll need to ensure that a recent version of APEX is installed. To follow along with the examples in this book, you will need APEX 4.1 or above. The following query identifies the current version of APEX installed on your database:

```
SELECT *
FROM apex_release
```

If you don't have APEX installed or need to upgrade it, you can download it from OTN: www.oracle.com/technetwork/developer-tools/apex/downloads/index.html. The download page has links to detailed instructions on how to install or upgrade APEX. If you are using apex.oracle.com, you do not need to install or upgrade APEX.

Development IDE

When developing plug-ins, it's highly recommended that you use a good PL/SQL and SQL IDE. SQL Developer is a free, Java-based, PL/SQL, and SQL IDE developed by Oracle. You can download SQL from OTN: www.oracle.com/technetwork/developer-tools/sql-developer/overview/index.html. SQL Developer provides syntax highlighting, allows you to quickly browse all the database objects, implement unit tests, and debug code. There are other third-party tools, such as Toad from Quest software.

A good text editor will help when creating and modifying web files such as CSS, JS, and HTML. There are many free text editors available such as Notepad++ (http://notepad-plus-plus.org).

Web Browser

APEX officially supports the following major browsers: IE 7+, Firefox 3.5+, Google Chrome 4.0+, and Safari 4.0+. You can use any of these browsers to develop plug-ins, but some may be easier than others.

This book assumes that you will be developing plug-ins with either Firefox 4.0+ or Google Chrome 11.0+. When using Firefox, Firebug (http://getfirebug.com) should be installed. Chapter 8 describes how to install and configure Firebug for Firefox.

Web Server

A web server is the gateway that allows your browser to communicate to the database and serve files to the client's browser. As part of the APEX installation process, you will have had to setup a web server.

One of the key components to developing certain types of plug-ins in APEX is the use of external files, such as JavaScript and CSS files. When working with external files, it is easiest if you can store them on an accessible web server and modify them directly.

Depending on your personal or organization's setup, you may not have access to a web server. Installing a local web server is not required for this book but is highly recommended if you don't have quick and easy access to one. Chapter 8 contains step-by-step instructions on how to install and configure a free local web server.

Summary

This chapter gives a high-level overview of what is and isn't covered in this book. Although not all types of APEX plug-ins will be covered, you will get a solid understanding of how they work. Once you've read through this book,you should be able to use what you've learned to create your own plug-ins, which you can share within your organization or with the APEX community.

■ ■ ■

CHAPTER 2

Plug-In Fundamentals

Plug-ins are shared component objects. Like other shared components, they are local to an application and can be made accessible (via subscriptions) to other applications in the same workspace.

The main part of a plug-in consists of PL/SQL code with JavaScript and CSS as complimentary code (when applicable). A plug-in consists of one or more PL/SQL functions. These functions can either reside in the database (in a package or a set of functions) or be included within the plug-in. There are specific headers for each type of function (i.e., they must take in a certain set of parameters and return a specific type). What happens in each function is entirely up to you, the plug-in developer.

Certain types of plug-ins can also leverage third-party web files, such as JavaScript and CSS files. These files can be stored in APEX or on a web server, or bundled as part of the plug-in. The PL/SQL code in the plug-in must explicitly load these third-party files.

Plug-ins also contain attributes that, like native APEX objects, allow developers to customize the use of the object. Attributes are either global or local. The PL/SQL functions have access to these attributes.

Creating a Plug-In

Before looking at all the plug-in options, you will need to create an "empty" or "skeleton" plug-in. An empty plug-in is just a plug-in with no code in it yet. Later chapters will discuss how to build each plug-in type in detail and will reference this section for the initial steps to create a plug-in. The following steps describe how to create an empty plug-in:

1. In the Application Builder, create an empty application with a blank page, Page 1.

2. Select the new application, and then go to the SharedComponents section. Under the User Interface region, click the "Plug-ins" link, as shown in Figure 2-1.

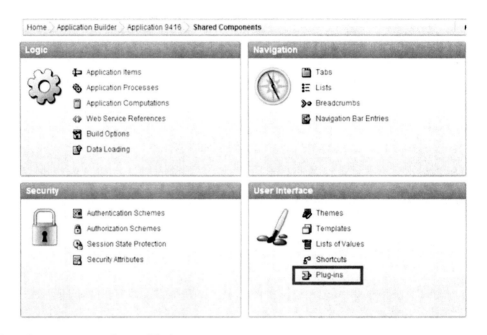

Figure 2-1. Shared Components "Plug-ins" link

3. The Plug-ins page displays all the current plug-ins associated with your application, as shown in Figure 2-2. Click the Create button to create a new plug-in.

Figure 2-2. List of plug-ins

4. Enter **Test** for the Name and Internal Name fields. Select "item" as the
    type, and click the Create button to complete creating an empty plug-in,
    as shown in Figure 2-3. All of the options will be discussed in the next part
    of this chapter.

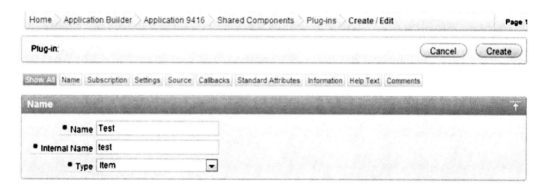

Figure 2-3. Creating a plug-in

Plug-In Components

It is important to have a good understanding of each of the options before building your first plug-in.
This section will cover all the available options or components involved in building a plug-in. If some
components seem a bit confusing, don't worry. They will all be used throughout the demos in this book.
To help follow along, edit the Test "empty" plug-in that you created in the previous section.

Name

Like most APEX objects, the Name section allows you to define the name and type for the plug-in, as
shown in Figure 2-3. The following fields are required in the Name section:

> *Name*: This is the name that other developers will see when they use a plug-in
> object. If developing plug-ins for the community, you may want to prefix the
> name with your company name.
>
> *Internal Name*: This is a unique internal name that is not visible to APEX
> developers. APEX uses the internal name to register your plug-in in an
> application. It's recommended that you use the reverse DNS name of your
> corporate website along with the plug-in name to help maintain uniqueness—
> for example, `COM.CLARIFIT.FROMTODATEPICKER`. APEX uses the internal name to
> determine if a plug-in is being installed or updated, so it's important not to
> change it once it's been released. Once the plug-in has been used in an
> application, the internal name cannot be changed.

Type: The type of plug-in that you're building; there are six different types of plug-ins: authentication, authorization, dynamic action, item, region, and process. Plug-ins can be run as part of the render, validation, or page process. Table 2-1 shows how each type of plug-in can be used in an APEX page. Once a plug-in has been used in an application, the type cannot be changed. The type cannot be changed because each plug-in type has a distinct set of attributes that will become evident in the Callbacks section.

The plug-in type determines when, and how, the plug-in will be used, as shown in Table 2-1. Plug-ins that can be rendered usually (except for authorization types) require HTML code to be sent to the browser. Validation executions happen once the page is submitted. Processes can happen while the page is being rendered or when the page is submitted.

Table 2-1. Plug-In Execution Options

Type	Render	Validation	Process	Comments
Authentication	No	No	No	Authentication schemes are used to determine if the user can access the application. As such it is not run on a page or component level.
Authorization	Yes	Yes	Yes	Authorization schemes can be executed for all APEX objects on a page. They don't actually render, validate, or process anything in the application.
Dynamic action	Yes	No	No	Since dynamic actions are only valid for the display portion of APEX they are only available during the render process
Item	Yes	Yes	No	Starting in APEX 4.0, page items may contain built-in validations that APEX developers don't need to explicitly define.
Process	Yes	No	Yes	Process plug-ins can be run as a page render process and page process. Usually it will be used as part of a page process.
Region	Yes	No	No	Similar to dynamic actions, regions are only valid for the display portion of an APEX page and thus are only available during the render process.

Category: Dynamic actions are broken up into various categories, shown in Figure 2-4, to help developers quickly find the appropriate dynamic action to use. The category that a dynamic action belongs to has no impact on the application. The Category option, shown in Figure 2-5, appears only when the Type field is set to Dynamic Action.

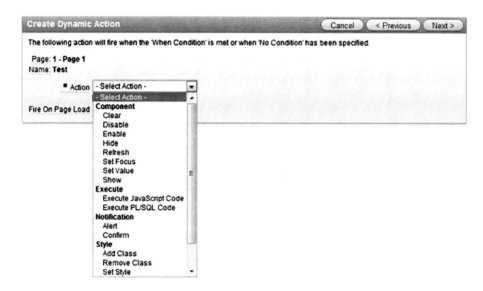

Figure 2-4. Dynamic action categories

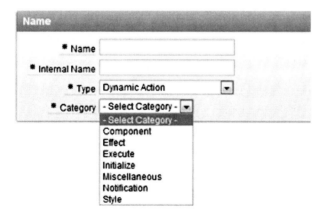

Figure 2-5. Plug-in category options

Subscription

You can share certain types of Shared Components objects in APEX with other applications within the same workspace. This sharing mechanism is called *subscriptions*. Subscriptions also allow you to subscribe to these objects. This means that you change something in your main object (referred to as a *master object*) in an application and *push* your changes to other applications that subscribe to the object. If you are unfamiliar with subscriptions, please refer to the manual.

The Subscription section, as shown in Figure 2-6, behaves exactly like other objects in APEX that support the same functionality. APEX allows you to create a master object. When the master object changes, you can push the changes to other objects that subscribe to it.

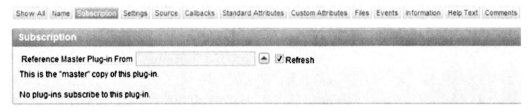

Figure 2-6. Plug-in Subscription section

Subscriptions may be useful if you have a plug-in that is used across multiple applications. If you need to update it, you can update the master copy and have APEX push the changes to all the other applications that subscribe to it. For more information about how to use subscriptions, refer to the APEX documentation.

Settings

The Settings section contains one option that is present for all plug-ins. This option is the File Prefix option.

> *File Prefix.* The File Prefix, as shown in Figure 2-7, defines the root directory to reference third-party files such as JavaScript and CSS. `#PLUGIN_PREFIX#` should be used if the files are included as part of the plug-in. You can also reference other APEX substitution strings, such as `#IMAGE_PREFIX#` and `#APP_IMAGES#`, as well as a webserver URL. If referencing a web server, you should include the trailing forward slash (/) to avoid having to include it in all references to files— for example: `http://www.clarifit.com/files/` instead of `http://www.clarifit.com/files`.

Settings

File Prefix	#PLUGIN_PREFIX#

Figure 2-7. Plug-in Settings section

Most plug-ins will also contain custom attributes. Application-level attributes will also appear in the Settings section. For example, as part of the item plug-in demo, you will create a special date picker.

Figure 2-8shows the custom application attribute Icon Location that is used as part of the plug-in. Icon Location is an application-level attribute that is applicable to all instances of the From To Date Picker in the application.

Figure 2-8. Plug-in setting with custom attribute

Source

The main part of a plug-in is contained in PL/SQL code. The Source section contains the following options, as shown in Figure 2-9.

> *PL/SQL Code*: The plug-in architecture allows you to either include the PL/SQL code as part of the plug-in or reference packages and functions in the database. If bundling the PL/SQL code as part of the plug-in, you'll need to include it in the PL/SQL Code text area. The PL/SQL code is called from the callback functions, which are covered in the next section.

> *Do Not Validate PL/SQL Code*: Like other PL/SQL and SQL regions, APEX gives you the option to exclude code from being validated when building your application. If this checkbox is selected, and code is put in the PL/SQL Code text area, it will be validated only at runtime. Unless there is a very specific requirement, it is recommended to leave this checkbox unchecked.

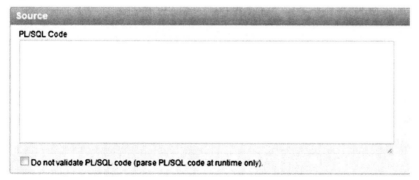

Figure 2-9. Plug-in Source section

Callbacks

Callback functions are the main drivers for plug-ins. Callback functions are PL/SQL functions that render items and regions, setup dynamic actions, execute authorizations and processes, validate items, and handle AJAX calls. Each of the plug-ins has a different set of callback functions. Table 2-2shows all of the required and optional callback functions for each plug-in type.

Table 2-2. Available Plug-In Callback Functions

Plug-In Type	Render / AJAX	Validation / Execution
Authentication	n/a Optional	n/a n/a
Authorization	n/a n/a	n/a Required
Dynamic action	Required Optional	n/a n/a
Item	Required Optional	Optional n/a
Process	n/a n/a	n/a Required
Region	Required Optional	n/a n/a

Plug-In Type	Session / Invalid	Authentication / Post
Authentication	Optional Optional	Required Optional
Authorization	n/a n/a	n/a n/a
Dynamic action	n/a n/a	n/a n/a
Item	n/a n/a	n/a n/a
Process	n/a n/a	n/a n/a
Region	n/a n/a	n/a n/a

Each of the callback functions passes in several parameters and returns an APEX_PLUGIN type. Click the help link to obtain the required function headers for each of the callback functions. Detailed information about each of APEX_PLUGIN types can be found in the APEX API documentation.

In the Callback section, you need to enter only the function name that APEX will call. The functions can reference either a package or function in the database, or a function that was provided in the PL/SQL Code region. The following is a list of all the callback functions and summary of what they do:

Render: The render callback function is used to render the element, load JavaScript and CSS files, and execute JavaScript code.

AJAX: If the plug-in requires an AJAX call, this function will handle it. Like standard AJAX calls, you can reference the `apex_application.g_x01 ~ g_x10` variables that are passed from the client back to the server as part of the AJAX request.

Validation: Starting in APEX 4, certain types of items have default validations. For example, on most items, you can select if a value is required, as shown in Figure 2-10, and enable these validations to be fired when submitting the page. It's important to note that the validation function will be run only if the APEX developer decides to as part of the submit process.

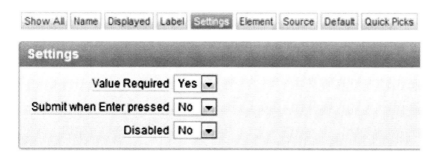

Figure 2-10. Page item Settings section

Execution: The execution callback function is the only callback function available for process and authorization type plug-ins.

Session sentry: The session sentry function is used to validate that the current session is valid. If left blank, APEX will default to its session validation function.

Invalid session: Function to call if session is deemed invalid

Authentication: This function will be run during the login process to ensure that the user's credentials are valid.

Post logout: Once APEX ends the user's session, this function will be called. It will determine where the user should go.

Callback functions can be a bit confusing when encountering them for the first time. The demos in the following chapters will use each of the function types just listed to help you get comfortable using them in your own plug-ins.

Standard Attributes

The Standard Attributes section contains a set of attributes that are related to the plug-in type. The following example demonstrates how modifying a standard attribute will affect the available options for an APEX object:

1. In the Test plug-in that you created in the previous section, scroll down to the Standard Attributes section, as shown in Figure 2-11, and ensure that all options are unchecked.

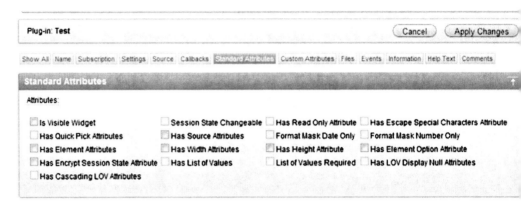

Figure 2-11. Item plug-in Standard Attributes section

2. Create a new item on a page (in this example, Page 1). Select the item type as Plug-ins, as shown in Figure 2-12.

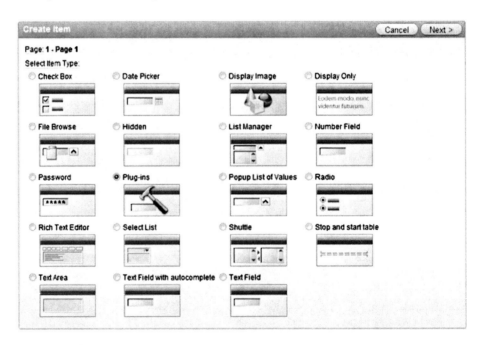

Figure 2-12. Create Item section

3. Select the Test plug-in, as shown in Figure 2-13, and click the Next button. You created the Test plug-in in the previous section.

Figure 2-13. Selecting plug-in

4. Enter the same values in Figure 2-14, and click the Next button.

Figure 2-14. Creating item name

5. Leave the Source page with the default values, and click the Create Item button to finish.

6. Edit P1_X. On the Edit Page Item page, there's a minimal set of options available for the item, as shown in Figure 2-15. Note that the Security, Configuration, and Comments sections were omitted from this figure.

Figure 2-15. Item with no standard attributes

7. Go back and edit the Test plug-in. Check the Is Visible Widget box, as shown in Figure 2-16, and click the Apply Changes button to save it.

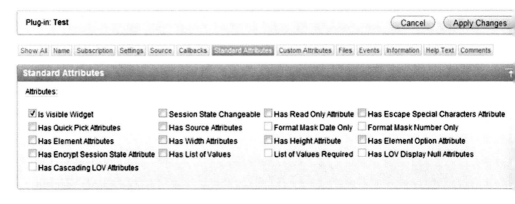

Figure 2-16. Standard Attributes option checked

8. Go back to Page 1 and edit P1_X. You'll notice that it now has more available options and some new regions. Figure 2-17shows the new options available for P1_X. Note that the Security, Configuration, Help Text, and Comments sections were omitted from this figure.

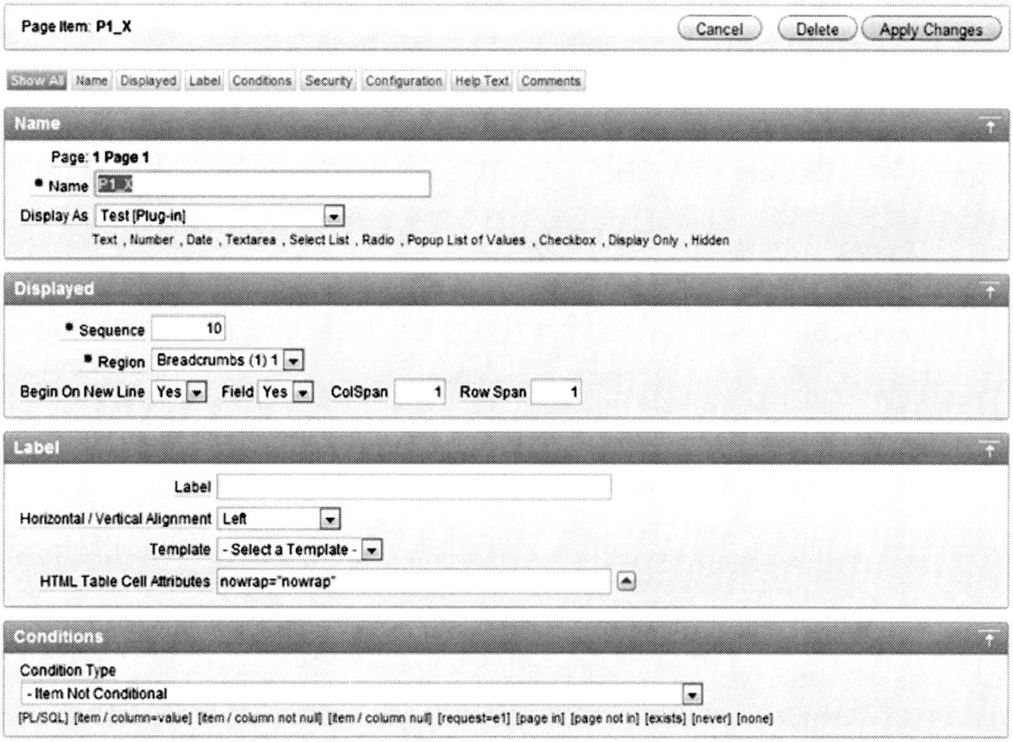

Figure 2-17. Item with Is Visible standard attribute enabled

If a standard attribute option is changed while a plug-in is already in use, the option is still part of the APEX object but not available for a developer to modify. For example, in the previous example, you enabled the Is Visible Widget option. Enabling this attribute allows you to enter a label for the P1_X item. If you entered a label for P1_X, and then disabled the Is Visible Widget option in the plug-in, the label would disappear from the P1_X item edit page. The label would still exist in the underlying table that stores P1_X information. It is important to remember this when modifying standard attributes once a plug-in has been used within an application.

Custom Attributes

Custom attributes allow you to configure options that can be referenced in your plug-in callback code. Custom attributes are already present in standard APEX objects. For example, if you create a password page item (see Figure 2-18), its attributes are "Submit when Enter pressed" and "Does not save state".

Figure 2-18. Password item custom attributes

There are two types of custom attributes. The following list describes them along with their differences.

> *Application*: Application attributes are attributes that are global for the plug-in across the entire application. They can be configured only in the edit plug-in page. For example, if you created a plug-in that uses a color attribute that should be consistent across the application, you would create an application attribute to store the color.

> *Component*: Component attributes are attributes that are specific for an instance of the plug-in. The password example that was previously discussed is a good example of component attributes.

You can choose to have APEX automatically replace substitution strings if they are used in the custom attribute value by setting the Substitute Attribute Values to Yes. For example, if a developer entered in &APP_ID. as a value and Substitute Attribute Values was set to Yes, then the value would be 100 (assuming the application ID was 100). If you set Substitute Attribute Values to No, then you must manually do string substitutions using apex_plugin_util.replace_substitutions.

To create either an application or component attribute, click the Add Attribute button, as shown in Figure 2-19. Attributes are stored as type VARCHAR2 in the database, so you will need to do explicit conversions if required. There's a limit of 15 attributes for each application and component attribute. The following subsections describe the available options for attributes.

Figure 2-19. Custom Attributes section

■ **Note** Some plug-in developers question why there are only 15 available custom attributes per plug-in. The APEX team restricted the number of attributes to make it simple for other APEX developers to use plug-ins. If you have too many attributes, other developers may get confused with all the options. Some plug-ins may warrant the need for additional attributes; however, it is up to you, the plug-in developer, to make some assumptions and choose default values. If users of the plug-in need to modify these default values, they can always modify them in the plug-in Source section.

Name

The Name section allows you to define how the attributes appear on the object edit page. The following list describes the available options shown in Figure 2-20.

> *Scope*: The scope determines the type of plug-in attribute. The two types of attributes were mentioned earlier. Once an attribute has been saved, the scope cannot be modified.

> *Attribute*: The attribute number determines the column in the table that this attribute is stored in. There's currently room for 15 attributes for each type. Since this is used to store the attribute value in a table, the attribute number cannot be modified once an attribute has been saved.

> *Display Sequence*: Like other APEX objects, you can control the display order of each attribute.

> *Label*: The label is the name displayed to the APEX developer using the plug-in.

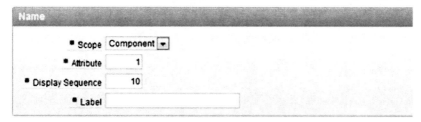

Figure 2-20. Custom attribute: Name

Settings

The Settings section, as shown in Figure 2-21, determines the attribute type. The options vary depending on the selected type. The available options are as follows:

> *Type*: The type of attribute will determine the rest of the available options in the Settings section. Implicit validations will occur based on the type. For example, if the type is set to Integer and a developer enters **abc**, an error message will be displayed. If you click the help link (i.e., the Type label), you will get a list of all the available types along with some additional information. Once a type has been saved and the plug-in has been used in the application, it cannot be modified.

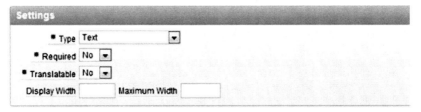

Figure 2-21. Custom attribute: Settings

List of Values

The List of Values section, as shown in Figure 2-22, will appear only if the type is set to Checkboxes or Select List. It allows you to define a static list of values for a developer to select a value from.

Figure 2-22. Custom attribute: List of Values

Default Value

If entered, the default value will appear as the value for the attribute when the plug-in is first created. If the type is set to Checkboxes or Select List and it is a required attribute, then a default value is required.

Condition

The Condition section is different than standard Condition sections for APEX objects. It determines the dependency for the current attribute with respect to other attributes for the plug-in. For example, suppose you had a plug-in that drew shapes and had the following attributes:

- Shape(square, circle)
- Length
- Width
- Radius

You would not want the Radius attribute to be displayed when the shape is a square. Instead you would conditionally display the Length, Width, and Radius attributes depending on the type of shape. Figure 2-23shows the Condition section for the Radius attribute.

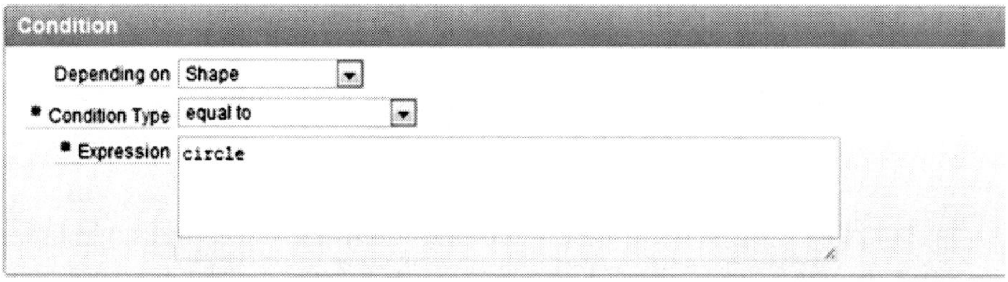

Figure 2-23. Custom attribute: Condition

> *Depending on*: This is the element that the current attribute is dependent on. In the example, it was Shape.
>
> *Condition Type*: The condition determines how to evaluate against the "Depending on" value.
>
> *Expression*: The value to compare against. If "in list" or "not in list" is selected, the expression must be a comma-separated list. The expression value is case-sensitive.

Help Text (for the Custom Attribute)

The Help Text section for a custom attribute allows you to provide some additional information for developers that are leveraging the plug-in. This text will never be displayed to end users, just developers. Like all other APEX help text, developers need to click the attribute label to see the help text. HTML code is allowed in the help text.

Files

The Files section allows you to include third-party files with your plug-in, as shown in Figure 2-24. If files are stored in the Files section, `#PLUGIN_PREFIX#` should be used as the File Prefix, as shown in Figure 2-7.

Figure 2-24. Plug-in Files section

The advantage of storing the files as part of the plug-in is that you don't need to worry about connections to other web servers, etc. If your application receives a lot of page views or you need to improve the page load time, it may help to store the file on a web server. When developing plug-ins, it helps to store the files on a web server that allows you to easily manipulate the files.

When using files, you should include a version number at the end of the file name. Including a unique version number for each file will make sure the browser uses the most recent version of the file rather than an older, cached copy. This concept is discussed in detail in Chapter 7.

Events

Events are custom JavaScript events that will be triggered by the plug-in. Some built-in JavaScript events that you may already know are onClick and onChange. Figure 2-25 shows the Events section on the plug-in page.

■ **Note** www.w3schools.com/tags/ref_eventattributes.asp contains a list of standard JavaScript events. jQuery handles these events in a very simple manner. For more information about jQuery events, see: http://api.jquery.com/category/events.

Figure 2-25. Plug-in Events section

Since events are tightly coupled with JavaScript code, they are available only for plug-ins that relate to page rendering: item, region, and dynamic action. Registering an event with a plug-in requires two components on the plug-in form:

> *Name.* Name is the display name that is shown to other APEX developers when they are creating a dynamic action.

Internal Name: This is the name that is used in the JavaScript code to trigger the event. APEX will lowercase the internal name automatically so you cannot use camel case in your JavaScript code that manages this event.

Events can be referenced by dynamic actions or by custom JavaScript code. If used by a dynamic action, they will show up in the list of dynamic actions. The following example demonstrates the relationship with dynamic actions:

1.   Edit the skeleton plug-in that you previously created at the beginning of this chapter. Scroll down to the Events region, as shown in Figure 2-25. Click the Add Event button.

2.   The page will reload. Scroll back down to the Events region, which now has a blank row for a new event, and enter **Dummy Event** for the Name and **dummy event** for the Internal Name, as shown in Figure 2-26. Click the Apply Changes button to save the modifications.

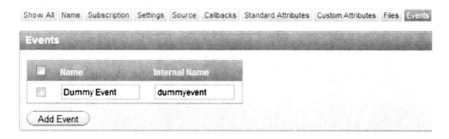

Figure 2-26. Plug-in Events section

3. On Page 1, create a new dynamic action by right-clicking the Dynamic Action tree element, and select Create from the context menu, as shown in Figure 2-27.

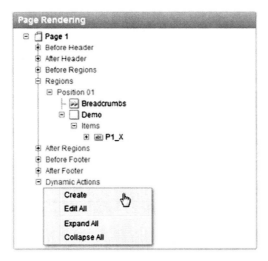

Figure 2-27. Creating a dynamic action

4. Select Advanced and click the Next button.

5. In the Name field, enter **Test** and click the Next button to continue.

6.   On the When page, expand the list of events. You'll notice a list of built-in events that are part of APEX. If you scroll to the bottom of the list, as shown in Figure 2-28, you'll notice Dummy Event in the list of events.

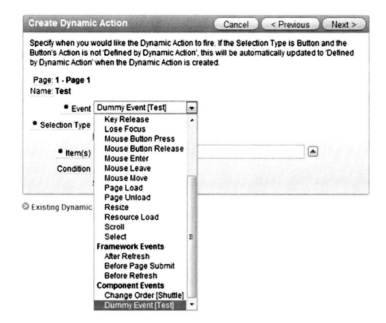

Figure 2-28. Dummy Event in dynamic action event list

7.   Since you don't need this dynamic action, hit the Cancel button to exit from the Dynamic Action wizard.

Events can be a bit confusing the first time when learning about them. Some of the demos will leverage events to help you understand how to build the additional functionality within your plug-in JavaScript code.

Information

The Information section, as shown in Figure 2-29, allows you to include some metadata about your plug-in. It contains the following fields:

Version: Like APEX applications, plug-ins contain version numbers. It is useful to maintain the version number to indicate if a new version of the plug-in is available.

About URL: You can put a link to a page that contains more information about the plug-in. When a plug-in is built for public consumption, developers tend to put their organization's web site on it. If it is built for internal use, you can put a link to a wiki page, which may contain more information about the business requirements for the plug-in, etc.

Figure 2-29. Plug-in Information section

Help Text (for the Plug-In)

It is recommended that you include any instructions in the Help Text section for the plug-in as a whole, as shown in Figure 2-30. The Help Text section can include both plain text and HTML markup. You can also include additional information, such as license information and documentation, in the Help Text section as well.

Figure 2-30. Plug-in Help Text section

Licensing

You can create plug-ins to give away, possibly in support of marketing your services. You can also create plug-ins to sell. The plug-in Help Text section mentioned in the preceding section is an excellent place to place your license terms, or at least to reference them.

Some plug-in developers prefer to publish their work under various *open source* licenses. There are many different open source licenses, each written with somewhat different end goals in mind. The following URL is a good source for information on the various open source licenses available:

`www.opensource.org/licenses/index.html`

If you choose to use an open sources license, you can just reference the license name and choose to include only the URL to that license in the help text for your plug-in. Users can follow the link to the actual license text if they are interested in the details.

Summary

This chapter covered all the components that make up a plug-in and introduced some of the APIs required to build a plug-in. In the following chapters, you will build each different type of plug-in, and that will make use of all the components that were covered in this chapter.

■ ■ ■

CHAPTER 3

Item Plug-Ins

Now that you know what plug-ins can do and their components, it's time to build your first plug-in. Don't worry if you're still a bit confused about how they work. This chapter will help answer most of your questions. Since it is the first plug-in in this book, everything will be defined in detail.

This chapter is broken up into four main sections. The first section, "Business Problem," describes what the plug-in is supposed to do. In the second section, you will build your first plug-in. This section will walk through each step and include some hints and tips. The third section, "Events," describes an advanced feature for plug-ins. The last section summarizes this chapter.

Note The plug-in that is built in this chapter was taken from a free, open source plug-in available from http://apex-plugin.com. This chapter will walk you through how it was built step-by-step.

Business Problem

One of the first mistakes people tend to make when creating plug-ins is to think about cool features and whiz-bang functionalities that their plug-in will have. Then they get so deep into the code that they eventually forget the problem that they're trying to resolve. The end result is either a failed attempt at building a plug-in or a plug-in that does a lot of things but not what it was initially intended to do.

Since there are a lot of moving parts with plug-ins, it's highly recommended that you take a step back and explicitly state what business problem you're trying to solve. This is a key step since you can always refer back to that statement and see if the work you're doing is going toward solving that business problem.

Note Explicitly writing down your business problem may sound like an excerpt from a project management book, but it is an important step for building plug-ins. Since plug-ins have so many components, it's easy to get sidetracked. Having a statement that you refer to will help keep you on track.

Example Scenario

The example in this chapter is built around the need for dynamic constraints on the values entered into a date field. The current date item allows you to select a min and max date, as shown in Figure 3-1. These constraints can be either static dates or references to a variable using the &ITEM_NAME. (substitution string) notation.

▪ **Note** For more information about the &ITEM_NAME notation mentioned earlier, and about different methods to reference variables, please read the following article: `http://www.talkapex.com/2011/01/variables-in-apex.html`.

Regardless of how you define the min/max constraints for a date field, they are calculated once when the page is loaded. As a result, the date constraints don't dynamically change as the user is working on the page.

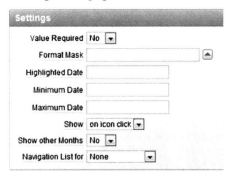

Figure 3-1. Standard date item settings

A classic example of when you would want dynamic min/max date constraints is when booking return airplane tickets. You normally select the date you're leaving on and then select the date you're coming back on. When you select the return date, you can't select any dates before the date you leave on, as shown in Figure 3-2. The current min/max date options in the standard APEX date picker don't support this functionality.

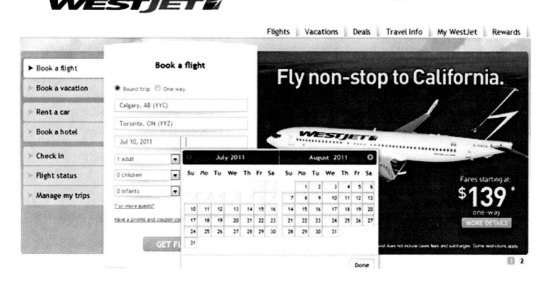

Figure 3-2. Dynamic min/max date when booking tickets

Solution Requirements

To get around the static min/max date issue, you're going to create a dynamic from/to date picker. The new date picker will have the following functionality:

- Restrict the *to* date when a *from* date is selected; for example, suppose you selected 20-Jan-2010 as your *from* date. When a user selects a date from the *to* date picker, he or she can't select anything before 20-Jan-2010 (i.e., the user can't select any dates from before 19-Jan-2010).

- Restrict the *from* date when a *to* date is selected; see the previous example in reverse.

- Allow developers to select when the calendar is displayed

- Support multiple date formats; date formats do not need to be the same for both the *from* and *to* dates.

- Back-end validation that dates are valid dates (if "execute validations" is set to yes)

- Back-end validation that *from* date is less than or equal to the *to* date

Building the Item Plug-In

Now that the business requirements have been defined, it's time to start building the new date picker plug-in. This plug-in will cover some of the most common features that you may encounter when building an item-type plug-in. If at any point you want to verify anything, an example application, covering all plug-ins in this book, is available on Apress's web site. (See the catalog page for this book at http://apress.com/ 9781430235033.)

■ **Note** This chapter's example will use external JavaScript files as part of the plug-in. To make things easier, the example assumes that you have read/write access to a web server that will allow you to modify the JavaScript files. If you don't have such access, you'll need to either obtain access or create a local web server. An example of how to install Apache, a free, open source web server, is covered in the Debugging & Tools chapter.

Creating the Plug-In and a Test Page

The first thing that you'll need to do is create the plug-in. The process is exactly the same as covered in the previous chapter except for the following changes:

- *Name:* ClariFit From To Date Picker

- *Internal Name:* COM.CLARIFIT.FROMTODATEPICKER

The plug-in type should be an item plug-in type. Once you have created the blank plug-in, the Name region should look like Figure 3-3. Everything else should remain the same with the default settings.

Figure 3-3. From/to date picker initial setup

The next thing that you'll need to do is create and compile an empty PL/SQL package in your schema. This package will be used to develop the from/to date picker item plug-in and the other plug-ins in this book. The code for the empty package, pkg_apress_plugins, is as follows:

```
CREATE OR REPLACE PACKAGE pkg_apress_plugins AS

END pkg_apress_plugins;
/

CREATE OR REPLACE PACKAGE BODY pkg_apress_plugins as

END pkg_apress_plugins;
/
```

▧ **Note** Storing the plug-in code in a package makes it easier/faster to develop. Once the plug-in is completed, you can store the code directly in the plug-in or move to another package.

Create a page to see how the changes you make in the plug-in affect the page item. Here are the steps to follow to do that:

1. Create a new blank page. Number it as Page 10, and name it From/To Date Picker.

2. Create a new page item and select Plug-ins, as shown in Figure 3-4.

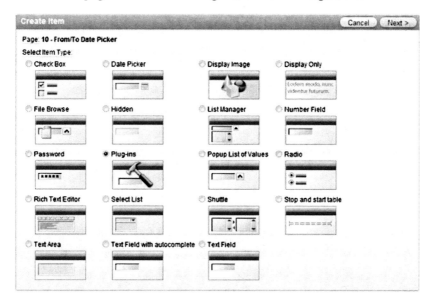

Figure 3-4.The Create Page Item wizard: Selecting the item type

3. Select ClariFit From To Date Picker and click the Next button, as shown in Figure 3-5.

Figure 3-5. The Create Page Item wizard: Selecting the plug-in

4. On the Display Position and Name page, enter the values, as shown in Figure 3-6.

Figure 3-6. The Create Page Item wizard: Selecting the display position and name

5. On the Source page, enter **DD/MM/YYYY** as the format mask, and click the Create Item button to complete the wizard.

6. Create another item by repeating steps 1 through 5 with the following changes:

    a. *Item name:* P10_TO_DATE

    b. *Format mask:* DD-MON-YYYY

Initial Configuration

Before writing any code for the plug-in, it is useful to configure the plug-in. There are usually two things that should be setup right away: the file prefix and the standard attributes. As you develop a plug-in, you can easily change these settings.

The file prefix defines the location for third-party files such as JavaScript and CSS files. The default value is #PLUGIN_PREFIX#, which references files that are directly attached to the plug-in. When developing plug-ins, it is usually easier to work on files that you have read/write access to. You can use a corporate development web server or a local webserver. This example, and all examples in this book, will reference a local webserver (covered in Chapter 8). It is assumed that you set the web server's home directory to c:\www.

The following steps will point the file prefix to a local directory for development purposes (*if using a different web server, change the URL accordingly*):

1. Create a directory called `c:\www\FromToDatePicker`.

2. Edit the plug-in and scroll down to the Settings region. Set the File Prefix field to `http://localhost/FromToDatePicker/`, as shown in Figure 3-7.

Figure 3-7. Settings: File Prefix field

Standard attributes define what standard options are available for the application developer to use. To start, check the options as shown in Figure 3-8.

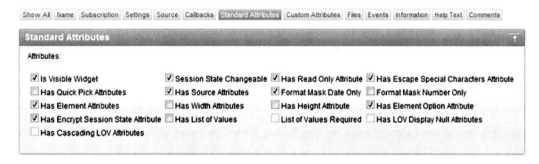

Figure 3-8. Choosing standard attributes

Including JavaScript Code

The next thing to do is add the JavaScript code to display the calendar and add constraints so the *from* and *to* dates are within a valid range. To display the date picker, you'll use jQuery UI date picker, which is the same tool that APEX uses for the standard date picker. The main difference is that you'll add additional support for the date restrictions.

▓ **Note** You can get more information about the jQuery UI date picker from

`http://jqueryui.com/demos/datepicker/`.

There are two components to adding JavaScript to a plug-in. The first is to write some JavaScript files with the plug-in. The second is to integrate the JavaScript code with the plug-in.

The first step is to write the JavaScript code to support the *from* and *to* date pickers. The easiest way to do this is to create a simple HTML file and build a proof of concept. This is a very important step since things can become complex when integrating into a plug-in. In order to save time, you will not need to do this step in this book; however, it is highly recommended when creating your own plug-ins from scratch.

▓ **Note** This section will cover all the JavaScript code required for the plug-in. When creating plug-ins, you will probably develop and modify your JavaScript code throughout the process rather than all in one go, as it needs to align with both the plug-in options and the PL/SQL code.

To create the external JavaScript file for this plug-in, create an empty file in c:\www\FromToDatePicker called jquery.ui.clarifitFromToDatePicker_1.0.0.js. Edit the file in your text editor, and add the following code (this is included in the downloadable files):

```
/**
 * ClariFit FromTo Date Picker for APEX
 * Plug-in Type: Item
 * Summary: Handles automatically changing the min/max dates
 *
 * Depends:
 *   jquery.ui.datepicker.js
 *   $.console.js  - http://code.google.com/p/js-console-wrapper/
 *
 * Special thanks to Dan McGhan (www.danielmcghan.us) for his JavaScript help
 *
 * ^^^ Contact information ^^^
 * Developed by ClariFit Inc.
 * http://www.clarifit.com
 * apex@clarifit.com
 *
 * ^^^ License ^^^
 * Licensed Under: GNU General Public License, version 3 (GPL-3.0) -
http://www.opensource.org/licenses/gpl-3.0.html
 *
 * @author Martin Giffy D'Souza - www.talkapex.com
 */
(function($){
 $.widget('ui.clarifitFromToDatePicker', {
  // default options
  options: {
    //Information about the other date picker
    correspondingDatePicker: {
dateFormat: '',  //Need other date format since it may not be the same as current date format
id: '',
value: ''
      }, //Value during page load
    //Options for this date picker
```

```
datePickerAttrs: {
autoSize: true,
buttonImage: '', //Set by plugin attribute
buttonImageOnly: true,
changeMonth: true,
changeYear: true,
dateFormat: 'mm/dd/yy', //Default date format. Will be set by plugin
showAnim: '', //By default disable animation
showOn: 'button'},
datePickerType: '', //from or to
  },

  /**
   * Init function. This function will be called each time the widget is referenced with no
parameters
   */
  _init: function(){
var uiw = this;

    //For this plug-in there's no code required for this section
    //Left here for demonstration purposes
    $.console.log(uiw._scope, '_init', uiw);
  }, //_init

  /**
   * Set private widget variables
   */
  _setWidgetVars: function(){
var uiw = this;

    uiw._scope = 'ui.clarifitFromToDatePicker'; //For debugging

uiw._values = {
shortYearCutoff: 30, //roll over year
    };

uiw._elements = {
      $otherDate: null
    };

  }, //_setWidgetVars

  /**
   * Create function: Called the first time widget is associated to the object
   * Does all the required setup, etc. and binds change event
   */
  _create: function(){
    var uiw = this;

    uiw._setWidgetVars();

var consoleGroupName = uiw._scope + '_create';
```

```
      $.console.groupCollapsed(consoleGroupName);
      $.console.log('this:', uiw);
      $.console.log('element:', uiw.element[0]);

    varelementObj = $(uiw.element),
    otherDate,
    minDate = '',
    maxDate = ''
          ;

      //Get the initial min/max dates restrictions
      //If other date is not well formatted, an exception will be raised
    try{
    otherDate = uiw.options.correspondingDatePicker.value != '' ?
    $.datepicker.parseDate(uiw.options.correspondingDatePicker.dateFormat,
    uiw.options.correspondingDatePicker.value, {shortYearCutoff: uiw._values.shortYearCutoff}) :
    ''
    minDate = uiw.options.datePickerType  == 'to' ? otherDate : '',
    maxDate = uiw.options.datePickerType == 'from' ? otherDate : ''
        uiw._elements.$otherDate = $('#' + uiw.options.correspondingDatePicker.id);
      }
    catch (err){
        $.console.warn('Invalid Other Date', uiw);
      }

      //Register DatePicker
    elementObj.datepicker({
    autoSize: uiw.options.datePickerAttrs.autoSize,
    buttonImage: uiw.options.datePickerAttrs.buttonImage,
    buttonImageOnly: uiw.options.datePickerAttrs.buttonImageOnly,
    changeMonth: uiw.options.datePickerAttrs.changeMonth,
    changeYear: uiw.options.datePickerAttrs.changeYear,
    dateFormat: uiw.options.datePickerAttrs.dateFormat,
    minDate: minDate,
    maxDate: maxDate,
    showAnim: uiw.options.datePickerAttrs.showAnim,
    showOn: uiw.options.datePickerAttrs.showOn,
        //Events
    onSelect: function(dateText, inst){
    var extraParams = { dateText: dateText, inst: inst },
            $this = $(this)
          ;
        $this.trigger('change'); // Need to trigger change event so that other date is updated
        $this.trigger('plugineventonselect', extraParams); // Trigger Plugin Event:
    pluginEventOnSelect if something is listening to it
      }
    });

    elementObj.bind('change.' + uiw.widgetEventPrefix, function(){
        // Sets the min/max date for related date element
        // Since this function is being called as an event, "this" refers to the DOM object and
    not the widget "this" object
```

```
      // uiw references the UI Widget "this"
      $.console.log(uiw._scope, 'onchange', this);

var $this = $(this),
optionToChange = uiw.options.datePickerType == 'from' ? 'minDate' : 'maxDate',
selfDate = $.datepicker.parseDate(uiw.options.datePickerAttrs.dateFormat, $this.val(),
{shortYearCutoff: 30})
        ;

      uiw._elements.$otherDate.datepicker('option', optionToChange,selfDate); //Set the
min/max date information for related date option
    }); //bind

    $.console.groupEnd(consoleGroupName);
  },//_create

  /**
    * Removes all functionality associated with the clarifitFromToDatePicker
    * Will remove the change event as well
    * Odds are this will not be called from APEX.
    */
  destroy: function() {
    var uiw = this;

    $.console.log(uiw._scope, 'destroy', uiw);
    $.Widget.prototype.destroy.apply(uiw, arguments); // default destroy
    // unregister datepicker
    $(uiw.element).datepicker('destroy');
  }//destroy
}); //ui.clarifitFromToDatePicker
})(apex.jQuery);
```

It is important to understand some of the techniques used. Here are some of the main points for the foregoing code:

- In the filename, jquery.ui.clarifitFromToDatePicker_1.0.0.js, a version number (_1.0.0) was added to the end of the file. This was done to prevent browser caching on updates to the file. The next time a modification is made to the file, just update the version number in the filename.

- The overall structure of the JavaScript file uses the jQuery UI Widget Factory framework. The jQuery UI Widget Factory framework is covered in the Debugging & Tools chapter toward the end of this book. This framework is not required when developing plug-ins, but it does make things easier to manage in the long run.

- The entire function is wrapped at the beginning so that you can use the $ jQuery notation. If the function was not wrapped, you could still use the $ notation but may run into namespacing issues. If you did not want to wrap your function, you could use apex.jQuery instead of $.

- The code was instrumented using Console Wrapper, a free, opensource wrapper for Console. Console Wrapper has tight integration with APEX and, by default, will be enabled only when APEX is run in debug mode. For more information, please visit http://code.google.com/p/js-console-wrapper/.

- options: Options that can be set by the calling function; some of these options will be setup as plug-in attributes so APEX developers can explicitly configure them.

- _create: This instantiates the jQuery UI date picker for the input element and sets the initial date restrictions based on other dates.

- plugineventonselect: In the _create function, there's a call to $(this).trigger('plugineventonselect', extraParams). This triggers a custom event that can be used when creating a dynamic action. An additional configuration (covered later) is required.

- _onChangeHandler: When a date is changed, this function will be called. It will change the min/max date restriction for the other date.

Since jquery.ui.clarifitFromToDatePicker_1.0.0.js references Console Wrapper, you will also need to copy the console wrapper file to c:\www\FromToDatePicker. $console_wrapper_1.0.3.js is included with this book, or you can download it from http://code.google.com/p/js-console-wrapper/.

For now you will not need to include the JavaScript file directly in the plug-in since you'll be referencing the copy on the web server. If there are any bugs in the code, it is much easier to debug. At the end of this chapter, you will bundle the JavaScript directly into the plug-in.

Adding Custom Attributes

Adding custom attributes can be done at any time while developing a plug-in. You'll tend to know some of the attributes right away and then add some additional attributes as you finalize the plug-in.

Based on the JavaScript code, there are two attributes that will be required: icon image location and when to show the calendar. To create the icon image location attribute, do the following:

1. Edit the plug-in and scroll to the Custom Attributes region.

2. Click the Add Attribute button, as shown in Figure 3-9.

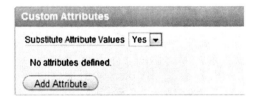

Figure 3-9. Adding an attribute

3. Fill in the Name region as in Figure 3-10. Since the icon image location will probably be the same throughout the application, it should be an application-level attribute.

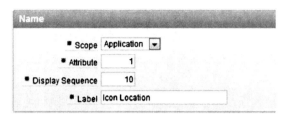

Figure 3-10. Custom attribute: Name

4. In the Settings region, set the Type field to Text, and Required field to Yes, as shown in Figure 3-11.

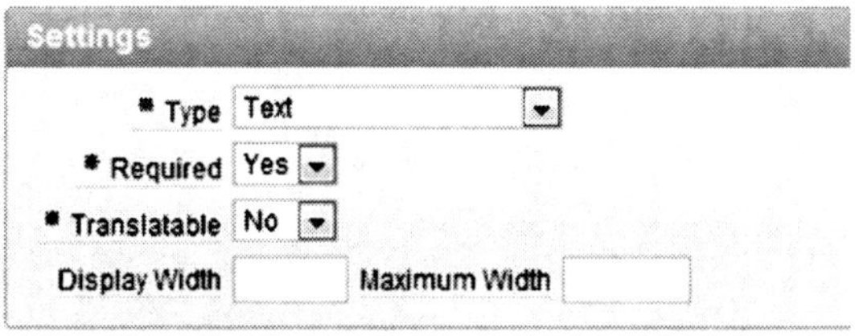

Figure 3-11. Custom attribute: Settings

5. In the Default Value region, enter **&IMAGE_PREFIX.asfdcldr.gif**, as shown in Figure 3-12. This will leverage the calendar icon image that APEX uses for standard date pickers.

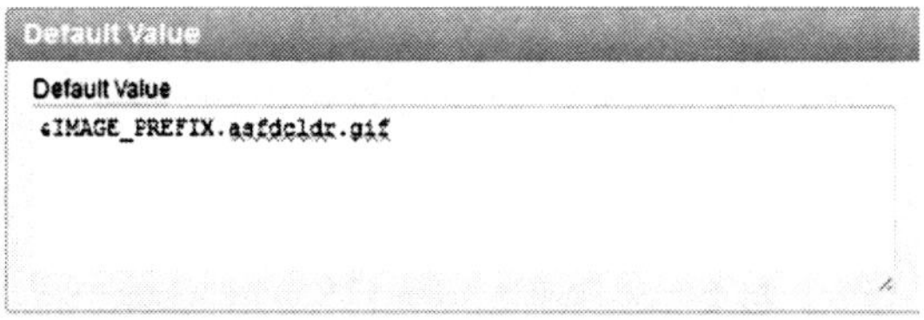

Figure 3-12. Custom attribute: Default value

6. Since this attribute is not dependent on other attributes, you do not need to modify the Condition region.

7. In the Help Text region, enter **Default image to use for calendar icon.** This help text will be displayed when a developer clicks the attribute label.

8. If you want, enter some comments in the Comments region. Once finished, click the Create button.

Creating the Show On attribute is similar to creating the icon image location application attribute, but with some slight modifications. The following steps outline the process. (Only figures for new steps are shown.)Figures for the other steps are essentially the same as before.

1. Edit the plug-in and scroll to the Custom Attributes region.

2. Click the Add Attribute button, as shown in Figure 3-9.

3. In the Name region, set the following values:
   Scope: Component
   Attribute:1
   Display Sequence:10
   Label: Show On
   Since this attribute may change for each instance of the date picker, it'll be a component-level attribute. The attribute number is unique based on the scope. Once an attribute has been created, the attribute number cannot be changed.

4. In the Settings region, set the following values:
   Type: Select List
   Required: Yes

5. The next logical step is to add a value for the list of values. The catch is that if you click the Add Value button it will submit the page and save the custom attribute. Since you set this as a required attribute, you need to define a default value first. In the Default Value region, set the default value to "focus".

6. You can now add values to the list of values. In the List of Values region, click the Add Value button, as shown in Figure 3-13.

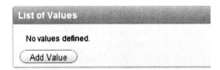

Figure 3-13. Custom attribute: List of values

7. Enter the values, as shown in Figure 3-14, for the LOV entry form. Click the Create and Create Another button when complete.

Entry	
* Sequence	10
* Display Value	Focus
* Return Value	focus

Figure 3-14. Custom attribute: Adding LOV value

8. Repeat step 6 for:
   Sequence: 20
   Display Value: Button
   Return Value: button

9. Repeat step 6 for:
   Sequence: 30
   Display Value: Both
   Return Value: both
   Instead of clicking the Create and Create Another button, just click the
   Create button.

When you go back to edit the plug-in, the new application custom attribute now appears in the Settings region on the plug-in page, as shown in Figure 3-15. If you edit P10_FROM_DATE, which uses this plug-in, you should notice the new Show On setting that you just created, as shown in Figure 3-16.

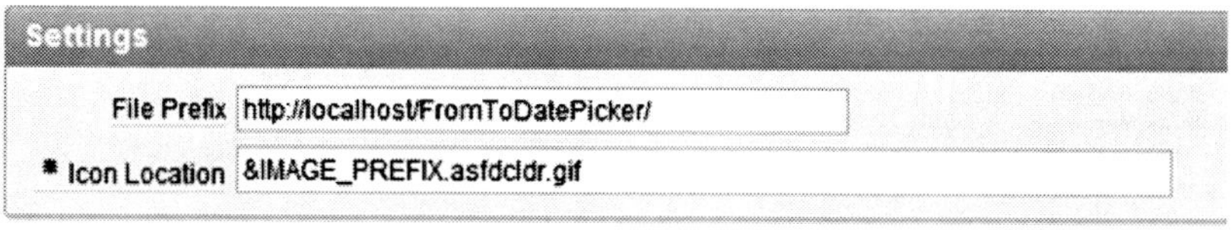

Settings	
File Prefix	http://localhost/FromToDatePicker/
* Icon Location	&IMAGE_PREFIX.asfdcldr.gif

Figure 3-15. Application-level custom attribute

Page Item: **P10_FROM_DATE**

Show All | Name | Displayed | Label | Settings | Element | Source | Default | Conditions | Read Only

Settings	
Value Required	No
Format Mask	DD/MM/YYYY
Show On	Focus

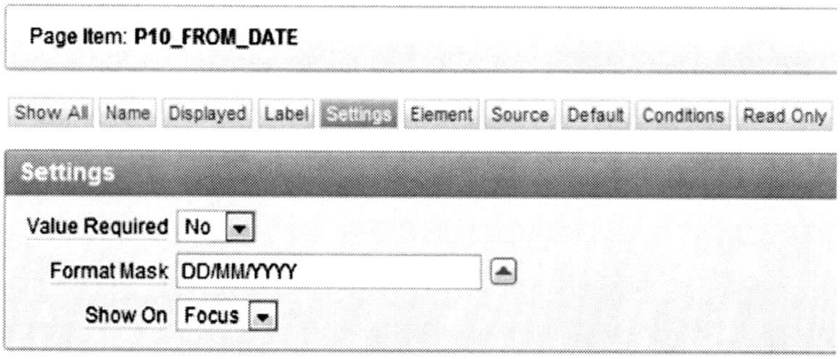

Figure 3-16. Component-level custom attribute

There are two other component-level custom attributes that need to be created for the plug-in. They are to select the type of date (from/to) and corresponding date item. To create these custom attributes, do the following:

1. To simplify things, only items that need to be changed from their default state or key fields will be listed.

2. Add a new custom attribute.

3. Name:
    Scope: Component
    Attribute: 2
    Display Sequence: 20
    Label: Date Type

4. Settings:
    Type: Select List
    Required: Yes

5. Default Value:
    Default Value: from

6. Check the Return To Page check box located in the top right corner of the page, as shown in Figure 3-17, and click the Create button.

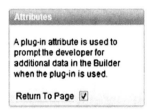

Figure 3-17. Return to Page check box

7. You will now need to add the following values for the list of values:

    Sequence: 10
    Display Value: From Date
    Return Value: from

    and

    Sequence: 20
    Display Value: To Date
    Return Value: to

8. Add a new custom attribute. This attribute will be to select the corresponding date item.

9. Name:
    Scope: Component
    Attribute: 3
    Display Sequence: 30
    Label: Corresponding Date Item

10. Settings:
    Type: Page Item
    Required: Yes

11. Click the Create button to complete this step.

If you go back and edit P10_FROM_DATE, you'll notice two additional attributes in the Settings region, as shown in Figure 3-18. If you click the Apply Changes button in the top right corner, you'll get a "Value must be specified" error, as shown in Figure 3-19. This happens since you couldn't define a meaningful default value when creating the Corresponding Date Item attribute. To resolve this issue, enter **P10_TO_DATE** in Corresponding Date Item. You should also update P10_TO_DATE and set Date Type to To Date and Corresponding Date Item to P10_FROM_DATE.

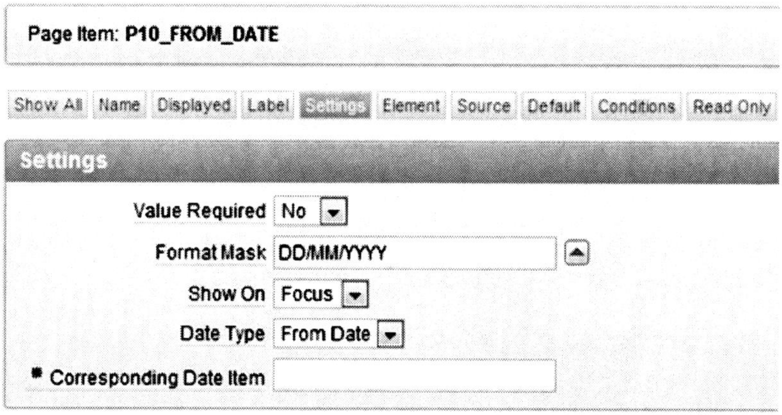

Figure 3-18. P10_FROM_DATE settings

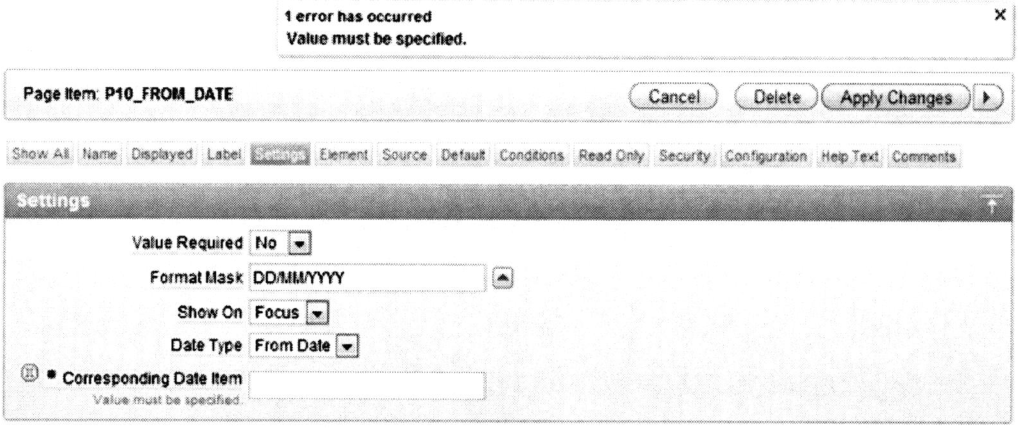

Figure 3-19. Missing setting value

> ■ **Note**   If you deploy a plug-in and need to add additional attributes, you should be aware of the consequences of having a required attribute with no default value. If no default value is set and the APEX developer upgrades the plug-in without modifying each instance of the plug-in, unhandled behavior may occur with negative results. As much as possible, when updating a plug-in, try to include a meaningful default value.

Rendering Function

Similar to the test plug-in that you created in the previous chapter, if you run Page 10, you will get the error shown in Figure 3-20. This is because no render function has been defined. In this section, you will define the render function so that the items display and work properly.

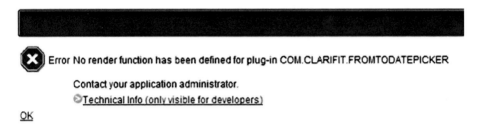

Figure 3-20. "No render function" error message

The render function is a PL/SQL function that writes the HTML code onto the page. For now store the render function in the package that you previously created, PKG_APRESS_PLUGINS. First create the entry in the package specification:

1. Open pkg_apress_plugins.pks in your SQL editor.

2. Edit the plug-in and scroll to the Callbacks region. Click the Render Function Name label to bring the pop-up help, as shown in Figure 3-21.

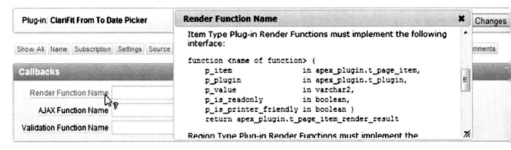

Figure 3-21. Render function help text

3. Copy the item type plug-in render function interface header and paste it into pkg_apress_plugins.pks, as shown in Figure 3-22.

```
 1   CREATE OR REPLACE PACKAGE pkg_apress_plugins AS
 2
 3 |   function <name of function> (
 4        p_item                in apex_plugin.t_page_item,
 5        p_plugin              in apex_plugin.t_plugin,
 6        p_value               in varchar2,
 7        p_is_readonly         in boolean,
 8        p_is_printer_friendly in boolean )
 9        return apex_plugin.t_page_item_render_result
10
11   END pkg_apress_plugins;
12   /
```

Figure 3-22. Item type interface

4. Name/rename the function to f_render_from_to_datepicker, and include a semicolon at the end of the return line so that the package specification can compile.

5. Compile pkg_apress_plugins.pks.

The next thing to do is to create a function in the package body and enter some standard code that is useful in all plug-ins. Copy the following code into pkg_apress_plugins.pkb:

```
  FUNCTION f_render_from_to_datepicker (
p_item                 IN apex_plugin.t_page_item,
p_plugin               IN apex_plugin.t_plugin,
p_value                IN VARCHAR2,
p_is_readonly          IN BOOLEAN,
p_is_printer_friendly  IN BOOLEAN )
    RETURN apex_plugin.t_page_item_render_result

  AS
    -- APEX information
v_app_idapex_applications.application_id%TYPE := v('APP_ID');
v_page_idapex_application_pages.page_id%TYPE := v('APP_PAGE_ID');

    -- Main plug-in variables
    v_result apex_plugin.t_page_item_render_result; -- Result object to be returned
    v_page_item_name VARCHAR2(100);   -- Item name (different than ID)
    v_html VARCHAR2(4000); -- Used for temp HTML

    -- Application Plugin Attributes

    -- Item Plugin Attributes

    -- Other variables

  BEGIN
```

```
      -- Debug information (if app is being run in debug mode)
      IF apex_application.g_debug THEN
apex_plugin_util.debug_page_item (p_plugin                    => p_plugin,
p_page_item               =>p_item,
                                       p_value                 => p_value,
p_is_readonly            =>p_is_readonly,
p_is_printer_friendly    =>p_is_printer_friendly);
      END IF;

      -- handle read only and printer friendly
      IF p_is_readonly OR p_is_printer_friendly THEN
         -- omit hidden field if necessary
apex_plugin_util.print_hidden_if_readonly (p_item_name           => p_item.name,
                                        p_value                 => p_value,
p_is_readonly            =>p_is_readonly,
p_is_printer_friendly    =>p_is_printer_friendly);
         -- omit display span with the value
apex_plugin_util.print_display_only (p_item_name           => p_item.NAME,
p_display_value       =>p_value,
p_show_line_breaks    => FALSE,
p_escape              => TRUE, -- this is recommended to help prevent XSS
p_attributes          =>p_item.element_attributes);
      ELSE
        NULL;  -- Need to fill this in
      END IF; -- f_render_from_to_datepicker

      RETURN v_result;
  END f_render_from_to_datepicker;
```

This code can be used for any type of item plug-in as it includes some debug code, print code, and standard variables. It does not include anything that will actually render the item in normal mode.

The render function returns a variable called v_result, which is of type apex_plugin.t_page_item_render_result. For more information, refer to the APEX API documentation.

The next step is to link the function that you just created with the plug-in. To link the render function with the plug-in, edit the plug-in and enter **pkg_apress_plugins.f_render_from_to_datepicker** in the Render Function Name field, as shown in Figure 3-23.

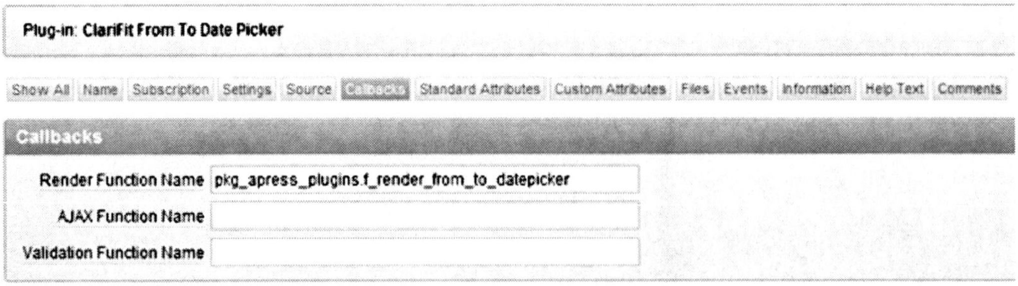

Figure 3-23. Adding render function

If you run Page 10 again, no errors should appear, like Figure 3-24.

Figure 3-24. From/to date picker with blank rendering

As Figure 3-24's caption states, the region is blank as nothing was displayed. The next set of steps will create the HTML input element so it displays on the screen. To do so, replace `NULL; -- Need to fill this in` with the following code:

```
-- Not read only
-- Get name. Used in the "name" form element attribute which is different than the "id"
attribute
v_page_item_name := apex_plugin.get_input_name_for_page_item (p_is_multi_value => FALSE);

-- SET VALUES

-- OUTPUT

-- Print input element
v_html := '<input type="text" id="%ID%" name="%NAME%" value="%VALUE%" autocomplete="off">';
v_html := REPLACE(v_html, '%ID%', p_item.name);
v_html := REPLACE(v_html, '%NAME%', v_page_item_name);
v_html := REPLACE(v_html, '%VALUE%', p_value);

sys.htp.p(v_html);

-- JAVASCRIPT

-- Tell apex that this field is navigable
v_result.is_navigable := TRUE;
```

To summarize the foregoing code, it prints an input element and then tells APEX that it's a navigable item. The attribute `autocomplete` is set to off on the input element to prevent a list of values being displayed when the user focuses on the field.

When defining the HTML code, mnemonics are used and then replaced for their appropriate values. This is a technique that John Scott showed at ODTUG Kscope 11 to make things easier when writing the HTML code. You do not need to use this technique, but it does make reading the code a bit easier. Of course, if your application needs to be as performant as possible, you may want to use a concatenated string and forgo the extra calls to the `REPLACE` function.

■ **Note** It is important to include the NAME attribute in the input element, as it is used in the form submission, and not the element's ID attribute. In general the ID is used as reference when the page is displayed and the NAME attribute is referenced from the server.

If you refresh Page 10, it will look like Figure 3-25 (note: if the item labels do not appear, then edit each item and add the label). You could submit the form, and APEX would process the items as a regular item.

Figure 3-25. From/to date picker with input elements

If you click either date field, nothing happens. They currently behave like regular text input fields. This is because you haven't linked the JavaScript code with the plug-in yet. Before including the JavaScript code in your plug-in, you need to create some variables to reference the custom attributes. Add the following code in the variable declaration section of the PL/SQL function:

```
...
-- Application Plugin Attributes
v_button_img apex_appl_plugins.attribute_01%type := p_plugin.attribute_01;

-- Item Plugin Attributes
v_show_on apex_application_page_items.attribute_01%type := lower(p_item.attribute_01); -- When
to show date picker. Options: focus, button, both
v_date_picker_type apex_application_page_items.attribute_01%type :=
lower(p_item.attribute_02); -- from or to
v_other_item apex_application_page_items.attribute_01%type := upper(p_item.attribute_03); --
Name of other date picker item


-- Other variables
-- Oracle date formats different from JS date formats
v_orcl_date_format_maskp_item.format_mask%type; -- Oracle date format:
http://www.techonthenet.com/oracle/functions/to_date.php
v_js_date_format_maskp_item.format_mask%type; -- JS date format:
http://docs.jquery.com/UI/Datepicker/formatDate
v_other_js_date_format_maskapex_application_page_items.format_mask%type; -- This is the other
datepicker's JS date format. Required since it may not contain the same format mask as this
date picker
...
```

Instead of using a variable name like v_attr_01 for application- and component-level attributes, use meaningful variable names. This serves various purposes. It makes things easier for other developers to modify the plug-in. There is also a chance that the attributes may change throughout the lifespan of the plug-in.

The other variables are there to manage the date formats. The from/to date picker allows for each item to contain different date formats. Note that it is highly unlikely that each item would contain different formats, but it is a possibility since the items are independent of each other.

To set the format masks for the dates, replace the section, starting with the code here. This code uses an undocumented function that converts an Oracle date format to a JavaScript date format.

```
...
-- SET VALUES

-- If no format mask is defined, use the system-level date format
v_orcl_date_format_mask := nvl(p_item.format_mask, sys_context('userenv','nls_date_format'));

-- Convert the Oracle date format to JS format mask
v_js_date_format_mask := wwv_flow_utilities.get_javascript_date_format(p_format =>
v_orcl_date_format_mask);

-- Get the corresponding date picker's format mask
selectwwv_flow_utilities.get_javascript_date_format(p_format => nvl(max(format_mask),
sys_context('userenv','nls_date_format')))
intov_other_js_date_format_mask
fromapex_application_page_items
whereapplication_id = v_app_id
andpage_id = v_page_id
anditem_name = upper(v_other_item);
...
```

Note Prior to APEX 4.1, you would need to include the following line in the foregoing code to handle substitution strings: v_button_img := apex_application.do_substitutions(v_button_img);. This is no longer necessary since you can declaratively tell APEX to replace substitution strings, as shown in Figure 3-9.

To integrate the JavaScript functionality, add the following code (excluding the "…") to the section, starting with the code shown here.

```
...
-- JAVASCRIPT

-- Load javascript Libraries
apex_javascript.add_library (p_name => '$console_wrapper', p_directory =>
p_plugin.file_prefix, p_version=> '_1.0.3'); -- Load Console Wrapper for debugging
apex_javascript.add_library (p_name => 'jquery.ui.clarifitFromToDatePicker', p_directory =>
p_plugin.file_prefix, p_version=> '_1.0.0'); -- Version for the date picker (in file name)

-- Initialize the fromToDatePicker
```

```
v_html :=
'$("#%NAME%").clarifitFromToDatePicker({
correspondingDatePicker: {
    %OTHER_DATE_FORMAT%
    %ID%
    %VALUE_END_ELEMENT%
    },
datePickerAttrs: {
    %BUTTON_IMAGE%
    %DATE_FORMAT%
    %SHOW_ON_END_ELEMENT%
    },
    %DATE_PICKER_TYPE_END_ELEMENT%
});';
v_html := replace(v_html, '%NAME%', p_item.name);
     v_html := REPLACE(v_html, '%OTHER_DATE_FORMAT%',
apex_javascript.add_attribute('dateFormat', sys.htf.escape_sc(v_other_js_date_format_mask)));
     v_html := REPLACE(v_html, '%DATE_FORMAT%', apex_javascript.add_attribute('dateFormat',
sys.htf.escape_sc(v_js_date_format_mask)));v_html := replace(v_html, '%ID%',
apex_javascript.add_attribute('id', v_other_item));
v_html := replace(v_html, '%VALUE_END_ELEMENT%', apex_javascript.add_attribute('value',
sys.htf.escape_sc(v(v_other_item)), false, false));
v_html := replace(v_html, '%BUTTON_IMAGE%', apex_javascript.add_attribute('buttonImage',
sys.htf.escape_sc(v_button_img)) );
v_html := replace(v_html, '%SHOW_ON_END_ELEMENT%', apex_javascript.add_attribute('showOn',
sys.htf.escape_sc(v_show_on), false, false));
v_html := replace(v_html, '%DATE_PICKER_TYPE_END_ELEMENT%',
apex_javascript.add_attribute('datePickerType', sys.htf.escape_sc(v_date_picker_type), false,
false));

apex_javascript.add_onload_code (p_code => v_html);
...
```

The first thing that the foregoing code does is load two different JavaScript libraries. The first is the Console Wrapper. As previously discussed in this chapter, it will allow you to include enhanced debugging in your JavaScript code. The second file is the custom JavaScript file that handles the *from* and *to* date picking functionalities.

Both of the file load calls include the file name, a directory, and a version parameter. The file name is the file prefix, not including the version number or the file extension. APEX assumes that the file has the `.js` extension. If it does not use the standard `.js` extension, you can use the `p_skip_extension` parameter. Referencing `p_plugin.file_prefix` for the directory is the best option as it allows APEX developers to define where the files are coming from rather than having to modify the PL/SQL code. That's it! You've officially built a functional plug-in.

To test that things are working, perform the following steps:

1. Go back to Page 10 (refresh if you already had it open). You'll notice that the two date pickers have slightly different widths, as shown in Figure 3-26. This is because the JavaScript code automatically resizes the fields to the appropriate widths based on the format mask. To change this feature, or make it configurable, search the JavaScript file for the autoSize option and change it to your desired size.

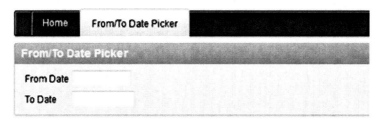

Figure 3-26. Date picker dynamic widths

2. Click in the From Date field, and select August 10, 2011 from the calendar, as shown in Figure 3-27.

Figure 3-27. From Date calendar selector

3. Click in the To Date field, and you'll notice that the calendar restricts you from picking anything before August 10, 2011, as shown in Figure 3-28.

Figure 3-28. To Date calendar selector

4. To demonstrate how the different custom attributes can change the item, modify P10_TO_DATE and change the Show On field to Button, as shown in Figure 3-29. Click the Apply Changes button to save your modification.

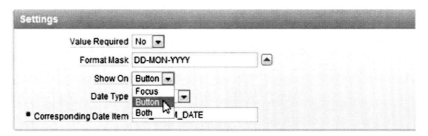

Figure 3-29. Altering custom attribute

5. If you refresh Page 10 again, you'll notice that the To Date field has an icon beside it, as shown in Figure 3-30. The calendar will be displayed only when the button is pressed.

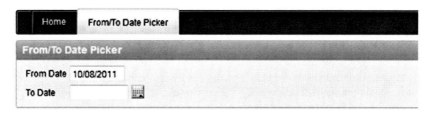

Figure 3-30. Modified To Date field

The JavaScript file that you created included a lot of debug/instrumentation code to output to the Console window. If you run the application in debug mode and view the Console window, it should look like Figure 3-31. Having this extra information can be very useful when resolving issues that you may encounter while developing a plug-in.

Figure 3-31. Console output

Adding a Validation Function

Now that the date picker is rendering the calendar correctly, we need to ensure that the dates are valid. Developers could manually create a validation for each instantiation of the plug-in item. This would require a lot of extra, redundant work. Item plug-ins allow plug-in developers to include validations as part of the item. As you can imagine, this can save a lot of time if the plug-in is used many times.

Before looking at the validation function, it's important to see what happens without a validation function. To simulate this, do the following:

1. Edit Page 10.

2. Right-click the From/To Date Picker region, and select Create Region Button, as shown in Figure 3-32.

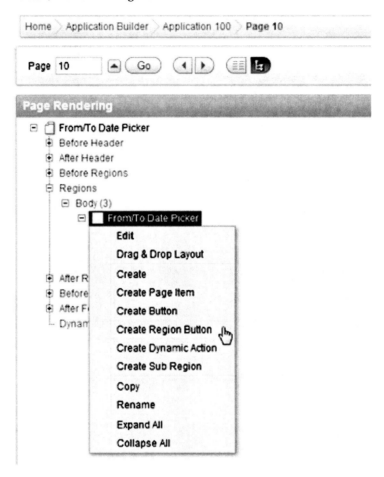

Figure 3-32. Create Region Button option

3.   Enter **SUBMIT** for the Button Name and **Submit** for the Label, as shown in Figure 3-33. Click the Next button to continue.

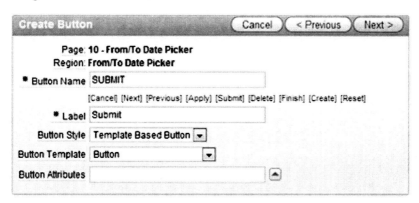

Figure 3-33. Create Button: Button attributes

4.   On the Display Properties page, set the Alignment field to Left and click the Next button.

5.   On the Action When Clicked page, leave the default values, as shown in Figure 3-34, and click the Create Button button to complete the wizard.

Figure 3-34. Create Button: Action When Clicked values

6. Create a new page PL/SQL process called Convert To Date to Oracle Date, as shown in Figure 3-35. Click the Next button.

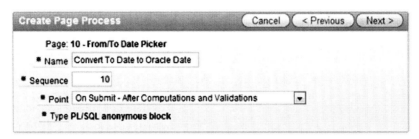

Figure 3-35. Create Page Process region

7. On the next page, enter the following code in the Enter PL/SQL Page Process text area. This code is some dummy code that will convert the text date into an Oracle date. It will fail if the date format is invalid.

```
DECLARE
v_format_maskapex_application_page_items.format_mask%type;
v_date date;
BEGIN

  -- Get format mask
  SELECT format_mask
  INTO v_format_mask
  FROM apex_application_page_items
  WHERE application_id= :app_id
  AND page_id= :app_page_id
  AND item_name = 'P10_TO_DATE';

  -- Convert text date to Oracle date
  -- This will fail if P10_TO_DATE has an invalid date format
IF :p10_to_date IS NOT NULL THEN
v_date := to_date(:p10_to_date, v_format_mask);
  END IF;

END;
```

8. Click the Create Process button to complete the wizard.

9. To test the new function and see what happens when no validations occur on the date item, run Page 10 and click the To Date input element. Enter **abc**, as shown in Figure 3-36.

Figure 3-36. Invalid to date

10. Clicking the Submit button will trigger the page process to run. You will get an error like Figure 3-37 rather than a user-friendly error.

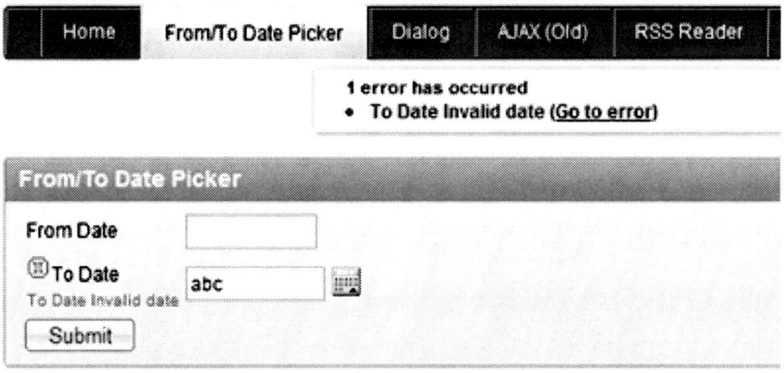

Figure 3-37. Invalid date error message

Going back to the plug-in requirements, there are two different validations that must occur:

- Back-end validation that dates are valid dates (if "execute validations" is set to yes)

- Back-end validation that the *from* date is less than or equal to the *to* date

The first step to creating a validation function is to get the validation function header and modify the package specification (pks) file. To get the validation function header, do the following:

1. Edit the From/To Date Picker plug-in.

2. In the Callbacks region, click the Validation Function Name label. This will display the pop-up help, as shown in Figure 3-38.

Figure 3-38. Validation function spec

3. Copy the spec header and paste it into pkg_apress_plugins.pks. Name the function f_validate_from_to_datepicker. The full function header should look like the following code block in pkg_apress_plugins.pks:

```
...
FUNCTION f_validate_from_to_datepicker (
  p_item   in apex_plugin.t_page_item,
p_plugin in apex_plugin.t_plugin,
  p_value  IN VARCHAR2 )
  RETURN apex_plugin.t_page_item_validation_result;
...
```

4. Modify pkg_apress_plugins.pkb and add the following code at the end of the package. The function shown here shares some very similar aspects when compared to the render function—for example, similar variable declarations and the debug information. Note that this function is not complete yet. v_result allows you to set the error message and some additional attributes. Refer to the APEX documentation for all the available options.

```
...
FUNCTION f_validate_from_to_datepicker (
  p_item   IN apex_plugin.t_page_item,
  p_plugin IN apex_plugin.t_plugin,
  p_value  IN VARCHAR2 )
  RETURN apex_plugin.t_page_item_validation_result
AS
  -- Variables
v_orcl_date_formatapex_application_page_items.format_mask%type; -- oracle date format
v_date date;
```

```
   -- Other attributes
v_other_orcl_date_formatapex_application_page_items.format_mask%type;
v_other_date date;
v_other_labelapex_application_page_items.label%type;
v_other_item_valvarchar2(255);

 -- APEX information
v_app_idapex_applications.application_id%type := v('APP_ID');
v_page_idapex_application_pages.page_id%type := v('APP_PAGE_ID');

   -- Item Plugin Attributes
v_date_picker_type apex_application_page_items.attribute_01%type :=
lower(p_item.attribute_02); -- from/to
v_other_item apex_application_page_items.attribute_01%type := upper(p_item.attribute_03); --
item name of other date picker

   -- Return
   v_result apex_plugin.t_page_item_validation_result;

BEGIN
   -- Debug information (if app is being run in debug mode)
   IF apex_application.g_debug THEN
apex_plugin_util.debug_page_item (p_plugin                => p_plugin,
p_page_item              =>p_item,
                                      p_value                 => p_value,
p_is_readonly         => FALSE,
p_is_printer_friendly  => FALSE);
   END IF;

   -- If no value then nothing to validate

   -- Check that it's a valid date

   -- Check that from/to date have valid date range
   -- Only do this for From dates

   -- No errors
   RETURN v_result;

END f_validate_from_to_datepicker;
...
```

5. To register the validation function, modify the plug-in and enter **pkg_apress_plugins.f_validate_from_to_datepicker** in the Validation Function Name field, as shown in Figure 3-39.

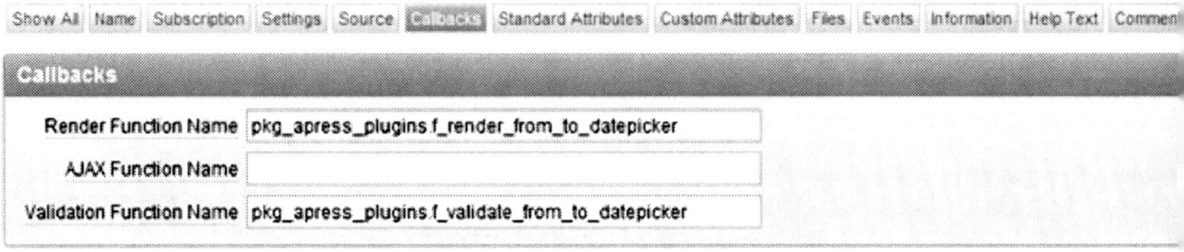

Figure 3-39. Registering validation callback function

If you run Page 10 and try to submit an invalid date, you'll get the same error that you saw in Figure 3-37. The validation function that you added was just a skeleton function. In the next few steps, you'll fill in the blank sections to include all the necessary code to add all the validations.

The first thing to do is exit the validation if the value is null. You can do this since each item has a general APEX attribute called Value Required, which will handle null entries. To ignore null values, add the following code below the comment.

```
...
-- If no value then nothing to validate
IF p_value IS NULL THEN
  RETURN v_result;
END IF;
...
```

The next check is to ensure that the current item's date is a valid date. This check will leverage the APEX dictionary to find the current item's date format and convert the item using that format mask. Add the following code below the comment.

```
...
-- Check that it's a valid date
SELECT nvl(MAX(format_mask), sys_context('userenv','nls_date_format'))
  INTO v_orcl_date_format
  FROM apex_application_page_items
  WHERE item_id = p_item.ID;

IF NOT wwv_flow_utilities.is_date (p_date =>p_value, p_format =>v_orcl_date_format) THEN
v_result.message := '#LABEL# Invalid date';
  RETURN v_result;
ELSE
v_date := to_date(p_value, v_orcl_date_format);
END IF;
...
```

In the foregoing code, when setting the error message, #LABEL# is used. If you do not include this, the error message will not include the name of the item. If the error message is displayed only in the notification area, it would be difficult for the user to decipher where the error occurred.

You can set the location of the error message in the v_result object by setting the display_location attribute. If you do not set this value, it will use the application's default display location. To set the default location, go to Shared Components Edit Definition and scroll to the Error Handling region, as shown in Figure 3-40.

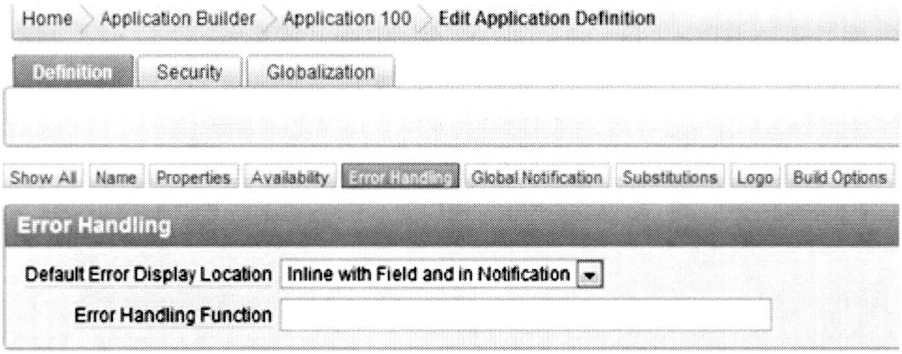

Figure 3-40. Modifying the Default Error Display Location field

There's still one last check to include in the validation function to ensure that the *from* date is less than or equal to the *to* date. In order to do this, you need to run the validation only once (i.e., not on both date item validations). In this case, the validation will check for a valid date range only on the *from* date item. Modify the code and add the following.

```
...
-- Check that from/to dates have valid date range
-- Only do this for From dates

-- At this point the date exists and is valid.
-- Only check for "from" dates so error message appears once
IF v_date_picker_type = 'from' THEN

  IF LENGTH(v(v_other_item)) > 0 THEN
    SELECT nvl(MAX(format_mask), sys_context('userenv','nls_date_format')), MAX(label)
      INTO v_other_orcl_date_format, v_other_label
      FROM apex_application_page_items
     WHERE application_id = v_app_id
       AND page_id = v_page_id
       AND item_name = upper(v_other_item);

v_other_item_val := v(v_other_item);

    IF wwv_flow_utilities.is_date (p_date =>v_other_item_val, p_format
=>v_other_orcl_date_format) THEN
v_other_date := to_date(v_other_item_val, v_other_orcl_date_format);
    END IF;

  END IF;

  -- If other date is not valid or does not exist, then no stop validation.
  IF v_other_date IS NULL THEN
```

```
    RETURN v_result;
  END IF;

  -- Can now compare min/max range.
  -- Remember "this" date is the from date. "other" date is the to date
  IF v_date>v_other_date THEN
v_result.message := '#LABEL# must be less than or equal to ' || v_other_label;
v_result.display_location := apex_plugin.c_inline_in_notification; -- Force to display inline
only
    RETURN v_result;
  END IF;

END IF; -- v_date_picker_type = from
...
```

■ **Note**   In this plug-in, the JavaScript code does a lot of front-end validation to ensure that the date ranges are valid, but it's still highly recommended to validate all data on the server using PL/SQL. A second check to validate all data at the serverside using PL/SQL is highly recommended so that clients will not be able to send deliberately incorrect data to the server.

The foregoing code does some straightforward validation. The thing to note is that it is explicitly setting the display location on the line that starts with v_result.display_location. The following steps demonstrate how the new error looks:

1. Run Page 10 and enter August 10, 2011 for both dates, as shown in Figure 3-41.

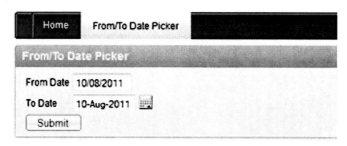

Figure 3-41. Same from and to date

2. If you try to manually modify the *to* date to be less than the *from* date, the JavaScript code will automatically correct the dates. To work around this, you'll need to remove the jQuery UI plug-in that is applied to one of the dates. To do this, open the Console window and run the following code:

```
$('#P10_FROM_DATE').clarifitFromToDatePicker('destroy');
```

The output from the Console window (if running the app in debug mode) should look like Figure 3-42.

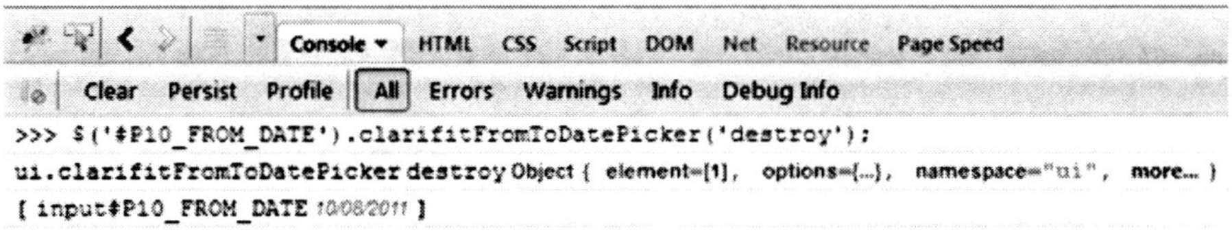

Figure 3-42. jQuery UI destroy output

3. You can now manually modify the *from* date. Set it to 13/08/2011, as shown in Figure 3-43.

Figure 3-43. Invalid date range

4. Click the Submit button. You should now get an error message like Figure 3-37,which checks that the date range is invalid.

Wrapping Up

Now that your plug-in is working properly, there are a few things to do before publishing it for others to use. If using the plug-in for internal purposes only, you may not need to change anything since you can reference a corporate web server and PL/SQL packages. These steps are there only if you're planning to release it publically or cannot guarantee that the APEX application will have access to a specific web server and PL/SQL packages.

The first step is to move the PL/SQL code from `pkg_apress_plugins` directly into the plug-in. The following steps will move the code from the package into the plug-in:

1. Edit the plug-in.

2. Scroll down to the Source region, and copy the functions f_render_from_to_datepicker and f_validate_from_to_datepicker from pkg_apress_plugins.pkb into the PL/SQL Code text area, as shown in Figure 3-44.

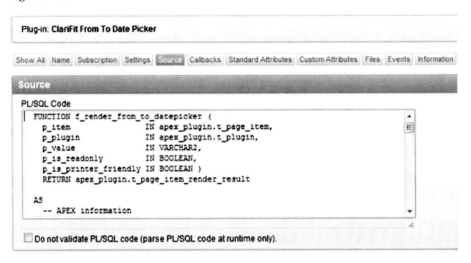

Figure 3-44. Embedding PL/SQL code in the plug-in

3. Go to the Callbacks region, and remove pkg_apress_plugins from the render and validation function names, as shown in Figure 3-45. Click the Apply Changes button to save your changes.

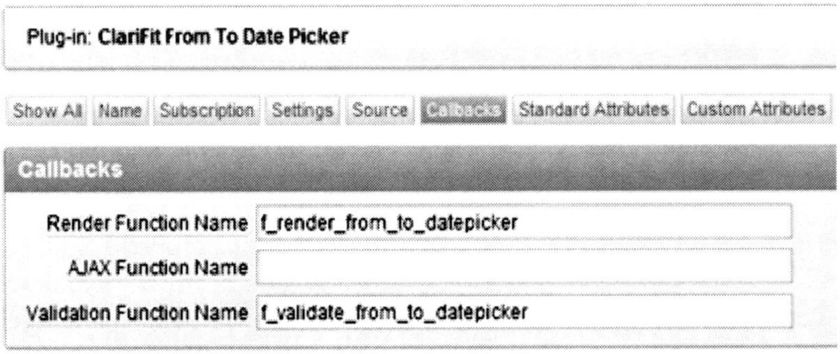

Figure 3-45. Updating call back functions

The plug-in is now running code that is embedded in your plug-in rather than from the package. You want to do this as one of the last steps since it can be more cumbersome and annoying to modify the PL/SQL in the plug-in rather than in a package where you can leverage all the features in a PL/SQL editor.

The last step is to embed the JavaScript files that were stored on a local web server. The following steps describe how to embed the JavaScript files in your plug-in:

1. Edit the plug-in and scroll down to the Files region, as shown in Figure 3-46, and click the Upload New File button.

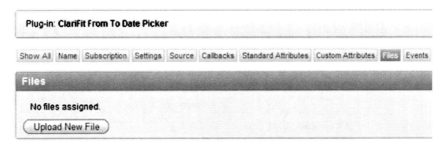

Figure 3-46. Plug-in Files region

2. This will open a new page. Click the Choose File button, as shown in Figure 3-47.

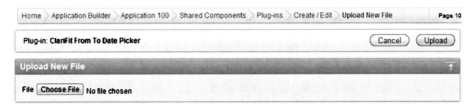

Figure 3-47. Upload New File region

3. Select `C:\www\FromToDatePicker\$console_wrapper_1.0.3.js`, as shown in Figure 3-48. Click the Upload button to upload the file.

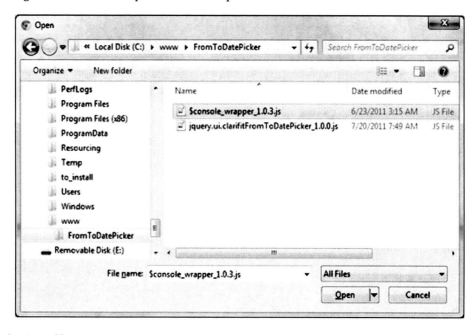

Figure 3-48. Selecting a file

4. Repeat steps 2 and 3 for `C:\www\FromToDatePicker\jquery.ui.clarifitFromToDatePicker_1.0.0.js`.

5. The Files region should now look like Figure 3-49.

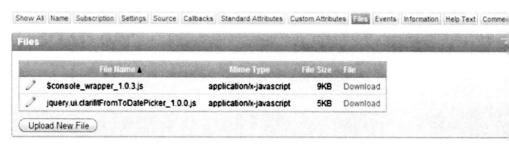

Figure 3-49. Files region with uploaded files

6. Go to the Settings region, and change the File Prefix field to #PLUGIN_PREFIX#, as shown in Figure 3-50. By changing the File Prefix field to #PLUGIN_PREFIX#, APEX will reference the embedded files rather than files on your web server.

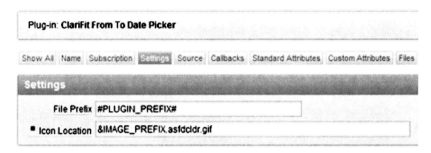

Figure 3-50. Plug-in Settings region

Events

Events allow you to declaratively link JavaScript events triggered from a plug-in to a dynamic action. In the JavaScript file, a specific line was added to handle custom APEX events, as shown here:

```
$(this).trigger('plugineventonselect', extraParams);
```

Events can be a bit confusing at first, so the best way to explain them is through a demonstration. The first thing that you need to do is register the event in the plug-in.

1. Edit the plug-in, and go to the Events region, shown in Figure 3-51. Click the Add Event button.

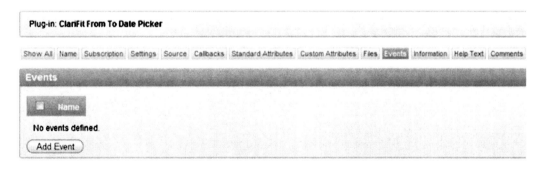

Figure 3-51. Plug-in Events region

2.   Clicking the Add Event button refreshes the page and adds a new row in the Events region. Set the Name to On Select Date and the Internal Name to plugineventonselect, as shown in Figure 3-52.

The name can be anything you want (i.e., it is used more as a display name that other developers will see). The internal name is the same name that you used in the JavaScript trigger function and is case-sensitive.

Figure 3-52. Registering the plugineventonselect event

3.   Click the Apply Changes button to save your modifications.

Now that the event has been registered with the plug-in, it can be leveraged throughout the application. The following example demonstrates how a dynamic action will use the plug-in.

1.   Edit Page 10. Right-click P10_FROM_DATE and select Create Dynamic Action, as shown in Figure 3-53.

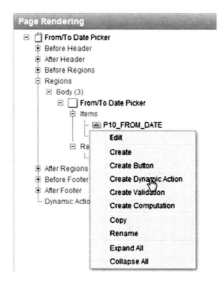

Figure 3-53. Adding a dynamic action

2. On the Implementation page, select the Advanced option, as shown in Figure 3-54, and click the Next button.

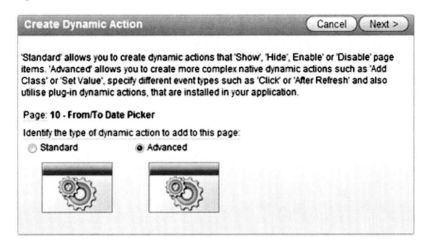

Figure 3-54.Dynamic action: Implementation

3. Enter **Display Selected Value** in the Name field, as shown in Figure 3-55. Click the Next button.

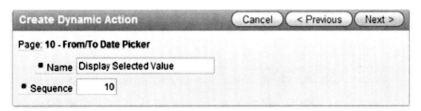

Figure 3-55. Dynamic action: Identification

4. The When section determines when the dynamic action will be fired. In the Event list, select On Select Date [ClariFit From To Date Picker], as shown in Figure 3-56. This is the event that we previously registered/created in the plug-in.

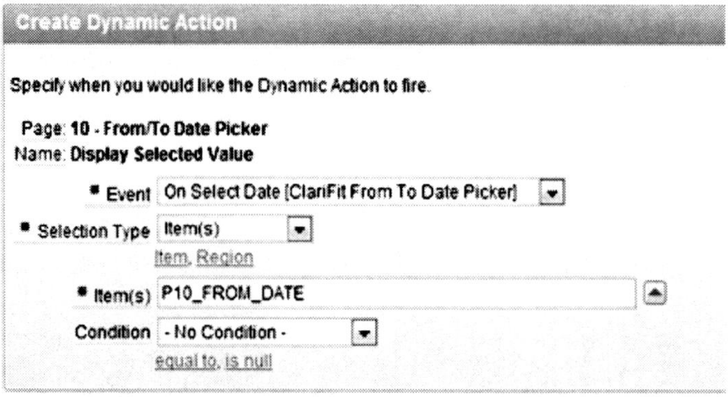

Figure 3-56. Dynamic action: When

5. In the True Action page, set the Action to Execute JavaScript Code. *Uncheck* the Fire On Page Load checkbox. In the Code text area, enter **window.alert('You selected: ' + this.data.dateText);**.Figure 3-57 shows the required change on this page. Click the Next button to continue.

Note that the variable dateText was defined in our JavaScript code in the extraParams variable.

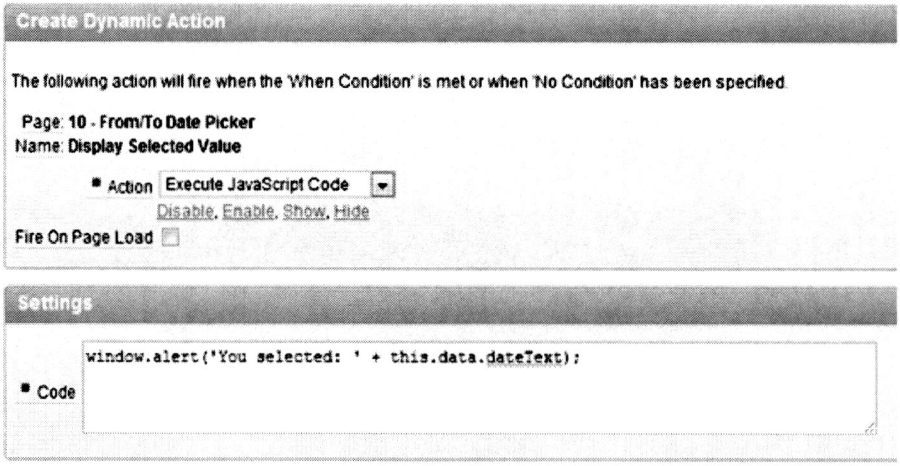

Figure 3-57. Dynamic action: True Action

6. On the Affected Elements page, do not select a Selection Type. Click the Create button to create the dynamic action.

To trigger the dynamic action, run Page 10. Select a *from* date, and an alert window should display the selected date like Figure 3-58.

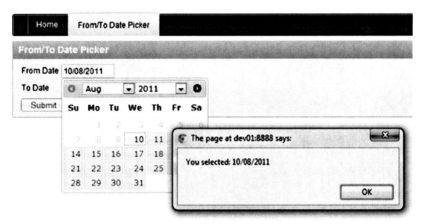

Figure 3-58.A dynamic action in action

This example highlights how to include events in your JavaScript, register them with the plug-in, and use them throughout the rest of your APEX application. Of course, you can do more elegant and meaningful things with events, but this example was kept simple to highlight how everything integrates.

Summary

This chapter covered many things, including callback functions, custom attributes, how to develop locally, and finally how to bundle a plug-in so it can be used anywhere. There are still a lot of things to learn about plug-ins, and they will be covered in the following chapters.

CHAPTER 4

■ ■ ■

Dynamic Action Plug-Ins

Dynamic actions were introduced to APEX starting in version 4.0. When they were first introduced, they were one of the most popular new features included in the release, alongside plug-ins. Dynamic actions allow APEX developers to declaratively define actions based on browser events.

This chapter will cover the basics of dynamic actions, including an example and how they work. If you are familiar with dynamic actions, you are still encouraged to read over the basics section, as the rest of the chapter assumes that you've covered this section. Following the background information, this chapter will build a dynamic action plug-in.

About Dynamic Actions

Since dynamic actions are relatively new to APEX, it is important that you have a good understanding of how they work. This section will describe what dynamic actions are and how they work.

The easiest way to explain a dynamic action is to create and use one. As an example, this section will walk you through creating a dynamic action that will print "hello world" on the screen. Follow along with the example on your own machine. Going through the simple process of creating this dynamic action will help you grasp what they are and why they are so useful.

To setup this example, you'll need to create a new page as follows:

1. Create a new blank page, Page 20, called Dialog, with a blank HTML region called My Region.

2. On Page 20, create a new region button called Trigger Dynamic Action. In the Create Button wizard, on the Action When Clicked page, set the Action field to Defined by Dynamic Action, as shown in Figure 4-1.

Figure 4-1. Create Button: Action When Clicked page

3. If using an older theme (pre APEX 4.1), you may get the same error as Figure 4-2. An ID is required on the button for APEX to link the dynamic action to. The following steps cover how to add an ID to the button.

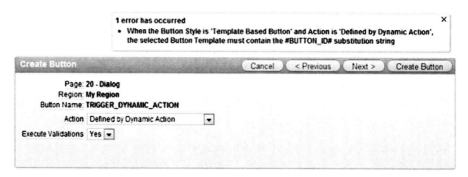

Figure 4-2. Button ID error message

a. Exit the Create Button wizard and go to Shared Components. Click the Templates link, under the User Interface region, as shown in Figure 4-3.

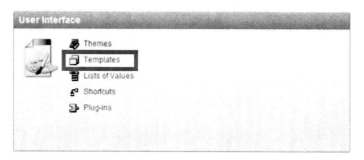

Figure 4-3. User Interface region

b. Select the default Button template (highlighted by the check mark in the Default column), as shown in Figure 4-4.

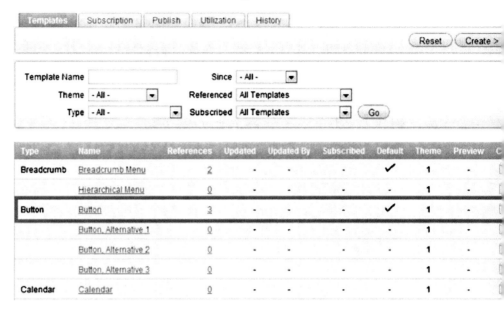

Figure 4-4. Selecting the default Button template

c. In the Normal Template region, change the code from

```
<button value="#LABEL#" onclick="#LINK#" class="button-
gray" type="button" #BUTTON_ATTRIBUTES#>
```

to

```
<button value="#LABEL#" onclick="#LINK#" class="button-
gray" type="button" #BUTTON_ATTRIBUTES# id="#BUTTON_ID#">
```

The only difference is that `id="#BUTTON_ID#"` was added to the tag.

d. Click the Apply Changes button to save your changes.

e. Repeat steps 1 and 2, and you should no longer get the Button ID error message.

4. Select the default options for the remainder of the wizard, and create the button.

5. On the Page Edit page, right-click the new button that you added and select Create Dynamic Action, as shown in Figure 4-5.

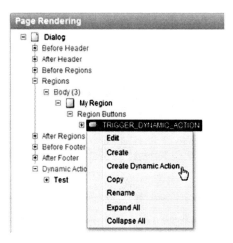

Figure 4-5. Create Dynamic Action context option

6. In the Name field, enter **Test**. Click the Next button to continue.

7. On the When page, ensure that the Event field is set to Click. Leave the rest of the default options, and click the Next button.

Note that the Condition option is not a "standard" APEX condition. Standard APEX conditions are executed while the page is being generated, which determine if the object should be rendered on the page. Dynamic action conditions are runtime conditions that will be evaluated in the browser when a browser event is triggered (in this case, the button being clicked). It will be evaluated each time the dynamic action is triggered.

8. Dynamic actions have true and false actions, which are based on the dynamic action condition. If no condition is specified, as in this example, only the true action will be run.

    The Action select list on the True Action page lists all the available actions to perform. They are grouped into categories. Categories are there for organization purposes only and do not affect a dynamic action's functionality.

    For this example, set the Action field to Alert, which is under the Notification category, as shown in Figure 4-6.

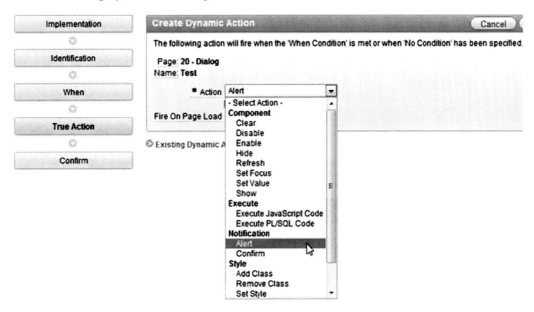

Figure 4-6. Dynamic action True Action page

9. *Uncheck* the Fire on Page Load checkbox, and enter **Hello World** in the Text box, as shown in Figure 4-7. Click the Next button to continue.

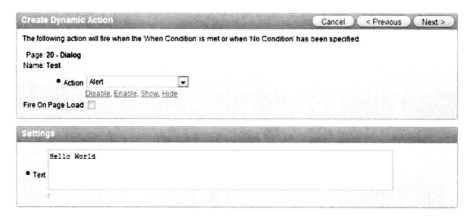

Figure 4-7. Dynamic action alert text

10. Click the Create button on the Confirm screen to complete the wizard.

11. Run Page 20, and click the Trigger Dynamic Action button. You should see a JavaScript alert window popup, as shown in Figure 4-8.

Figure 4-8. JavaScript alert window

How Dynamic Actions Work

As you can now see, it's really easy to use dynamic actions. But what actually happens behind the scenes? This section will discuss in detail how dynamic actions work. It's important to fully understand how they work, as you'll need to know this information when creating your own dynamic actions.

Dynamic actions can be broken up into two sections: drivers and actions. Drivers define *when* the dynamic action should be executed, and actions define *what* action should be run. Figure 4-9 is a flowchart of how a dynamic action works.

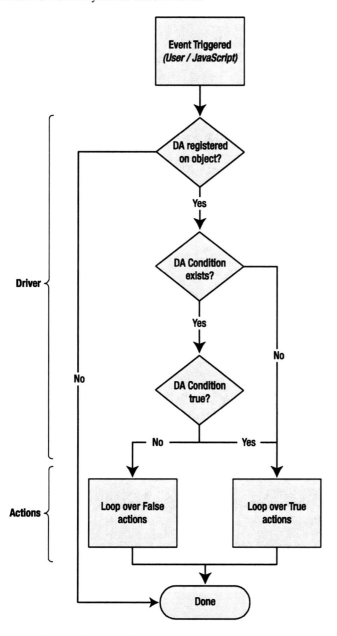

Figure 4-9. Dynamic action flowchart

In the previous example, the driver was the button click. Since there was no condition, the only action was showing the alert message box. When you create a dynamic action plug-in, you're actually creating something that will be run as an action.

Since dynamic actions are run on the front end, all the information that the action needs to perform is actually available when the action is executed. To demonstrate the available information, modify the Test dynamic action that you previously created:

1. On the Page 20 edit page, right-click the Alert action and select Edit from the context menu, as shown in Figure 4-10.

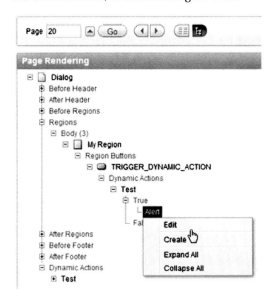

Figure 4-10. Edit Alert action

2. In the Identification region, change the Action field from Alert to Execute JavaScript Code, as shown in Figure 4-11. When doing so, you'll notice that a new region appears called Affected Elements.

Figure 4-11. Action Identification region

3. In the Execution Options region, *uncheck* the Fire On Page Load box.

4. In the Settings region, enter the following into the Code text area:

```
console.log(this);
```

5. Configure the Affected Elements region as shown in Figure 4-12.

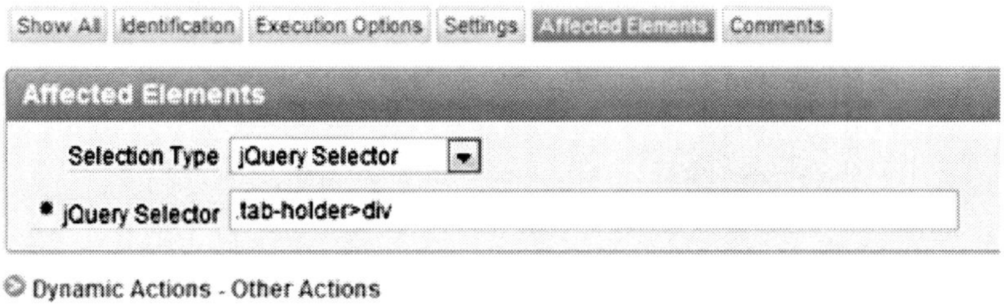

Figure 4-12. Action Affected Elements region

Affected Elements allows an APEX developer to select which elements on the page will be affected by the action. In this example, it will be all the tabs on the page; however, since the JavaScript code is just displaying an object, nothing will actually happen to the tabs.

6. Click the Apply Changes button to save your modifications.

7. Run Page 20, and open the Console window in Firefox. You can also view the console output in other browsers, such as Google Chrome or Safari. Viewing the console output in Firefox is a popular technique among developers as it offers a lot of details and additional third-party plug-ins/tools to help speed up development.

■ **Note** If you are unfamiliar with the browser console, Chapter 7describes it in detail.

---

8. Click the Trigger Dynamic Action button. Figure 4-13 shows what the Console window is currently displaying.

Figure 4-13. Firefox Console window

9. If you drill down on the Object hyperlink (which represents the this dynamic action object), you will see the following objects:

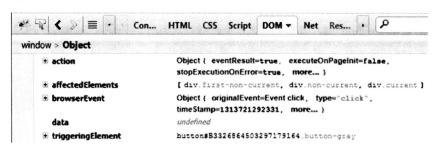

Figure 4-14. Dynamic action this *object*

The dynamic action this object contains five elements: action, affectedElements, browserEvent, data, and triggeringElement. The following list describes each of these elements:

action: The action element contains a list of attributes that describe the action as shown in Figure 4-15. The action, affectedElements, affectedElementsType, affectedRegionId, eventResult, executeOnPageInit, and stopExecutionOnError attributes are automatically set by APEX. In the PL/SQL code that generates the action plug-in, you can define the ajaxIdentifier as well as attributes 01~15. Note that these attributes are *not* the same as the custom attributes that you create as part of the plug-in. They are defined directly within the plug-in PL/SQL code. This will be covered in detail in the example plug-in later in this chapter.

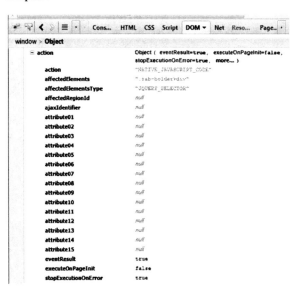

Figure 4-15. Dynamic action this*—action*

affectedElements:affectedElements is an array of elements that should be modified/used by the action. In this example, it is the three tabs at the top of the page, which represent the three elements (0, 1, and 2) in the array, as shown in Figure 4-16. This means that in your JavaScript code you should reference the affectedElementsarray rather than hard-code objects that should be modified.

Referencing the affectedElements object rather than a hard-coded value is one of the toughest things to get over when first working with dynamic actions. It does take some getting used to, but you should be comfortable with this notion after a while of working with dynamic actions.

Figure 4-16. Dynamic action this—affectedElements

browserEvent: The browserEvent attribute is the event that triggered the dynamic action to fire. In Figure 4-17, you can see that the element that caused the dynamic action to fire was the button.

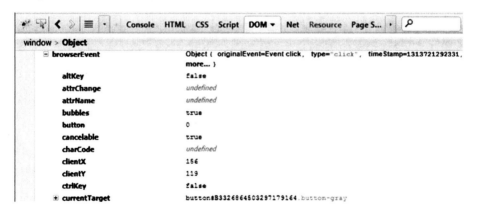

Figure 4-17. Dynamic action this—browserEvent

`browserEvent.currentTarget`: This represents the target element to listen onthat was defined by the APEX developer.`browserEvent.target` (not shown in Figure 4-17) represents the exact object that triggered the event. The difference between the two is subtle, and in this example they appear to be the same, but there is a difference. Suppose you change the driver for the dynamic action from a click of the button to a click of the region, as shown in Figure 4-18. Run the page, and click the Trigger Dynamic Action button. The `browserEvent.currentTarget` would be the div element (representing the region), and the `browserEvent.target` would be the button element (representing the exact object that was clicked).

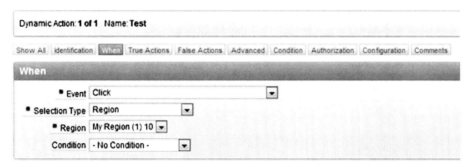

Figure 4-18. Modifying the dynamic action driver

`browserEvent.type`*(not shown in Figure 4-17)*:This highlights that it was a click event that triggered this dynamic action.

`data`: The `data` attribute contains additional data that can be passed by the event handler. An example of this was covered in the previous chapter in the "Events" section.

`triggeringElement`: `triggeringElement` is the DOM object that the dynamic action listener was applied to. This is the same thing as `browserEvent.currentTarget`.

The dynamic action `this` object is a very important object since the entire JavaScript portion of the dynamic action relies on its information. In the following example, you'll use some of the elements discussed earlier in your dynamic action. If you get confused with some of the JavaScript code, you should come back to review this section.

Example Business Problem

When creating an application, developers need to create pop-up windows for users to view and modify data. Since some browsers prevent web pages from using traditional pop-up windows (and they're annoying), you need to create a dialog/modal pop-up window. An example of such a window is the label help dialog window in APEX, as shown in Figure 4-19.

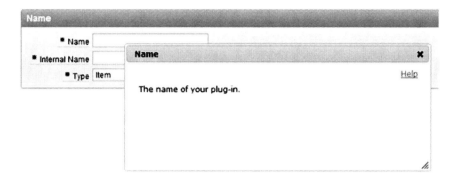

Figure 4-19. APEX label help dialog window

The following is a list of requirements for this dynamic action plug-in:

- Allow for modal and non-modal dialog windows.

- Dialog window can be moved around the page by the user.

- Support multiple dialog windows at the same time.

- Dialog window must be selected for Region, DOM object, or jQuery Selector.

- For modal windows, background color and opacity must be the same across the entire application.

- Ability to hide the dialog window on page load (i.e., user wants to see the information only as a modal window)

- Allow the end user to hit the ESC key to close the modal window.

- Option to restore the dialog window to its previous non-dialog window state—for example, if it was hidden before, it should be hidden after.

Building the Dynamic Action Plug-In

Now that the business requirements have been defined, you can start creating the dynamic action plug-in. To start, create a new plug-in with the attributes listed here. Follow the same process as in the preceding chapter. Once you are finished, click the Create button to save the plug-in.

- *Name*: ClariFit Dialog

- *Internal Name*: COM.CLARIFIT.APEXPLUGIN.APEX_DIALOG

- *Type*: Dynamic Action

- *Category*: Effect

Again, the category has no real impact on the plug-in. All it does is control where the dynamic action is listed when a developer is implementing a dynamic action.

■ **Note** Some of the steps that were covered in detail in the previous chapter are common to both types of plug-ins. The following process will not include screenshots for those common steps.

Initial Configuration and Setup

Just like the first plug-in that you created, there are some housekeeping items that you need to perform. The first is to create a directory on your web server that will host the necessary web files while developing this application and modify the plug-in file prefix.

1. Create a directory called `c:\www\ApexDialog`.

2. Modify the plug-in. In the Settings region, set the File Prefix field to `http://localhost/ApexDialog/`.

3. Click the Apply Changes button to save your changes.

Before creating a test scenario on Page 20, you will need to configure the standard attributes for this plug-in. Referring to the requirements, the affected elements for this plug-in must be selected. They can be only for Region, DOM object, or jQuery Selectors. To meet these requirements, modify the plug-in and set the standard attributes options as in Figure 4-20.

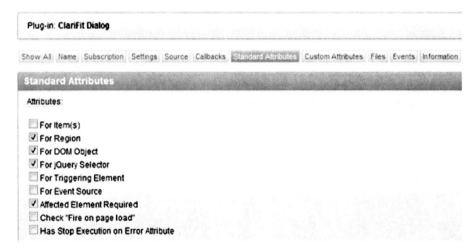

Figure 4-20. Plug-in standard attributes

As with all plug-ins, you'll need to reference a PL/SQL function(s) to manage the plug-in. The following steps will define the PL/SQL function for the plug-in and create a corresponding empty PL/SQL function in `pkg_apress_plugins`. The code for the function will be covered later on in this chapter.

1. Modify the plug-in. In the Callbacks region,set the Render Function Namefield to `pkg_apress_plugins.f_render_dialog`. Since this plug-in does not require any AJAX calls, you can leave the AJAX Function Name field empty.

2. The next thing to do is to define and create an empty PL/SQL function. To obtain the function spec, click the Render Function Name label. Scroll down to the bottom of the help text, and copy the function header information, as shown in Figure 4-21.

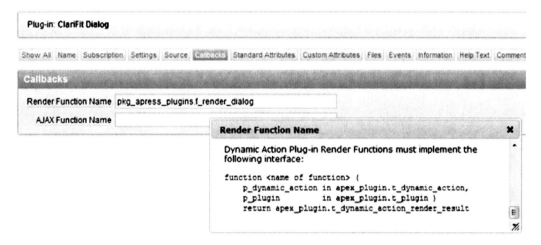

Figure 4-21. Render Function Name help

3. Modify the package spec for `pkg_apress_plugins`, and paste the code at the end. Name the function `f_render_dialog`. In SQL Developer, it should look like Figure 4-22(note that the other functions have been collapsed).

```
CREATE OR REPLACE PACKAGE pkg_apress_plugins AS

    FUNCTION f_render_from_to_datepicker (...

    FUNCTION f_validate_from_to_datepicker (...

    FUNCTION f_render_dialog (
        p_dynamic_action IN apex_plugin.t_dynamic_action,
        p_plugin         IN apex_plugin.t_plugin )
        RETURN apex_plugin.t_dynamic_action_render_result;

END pkg_apress_plugins;
/
```

Figure 4-22.`pkg_apress_plugins.f_render_dialog`package spec

4. Create the function **f_render_dialog** in the package body, which simply returns an empty result variable, as shown in Figure 4-23 (note that the other functions have been collapsed). You will fill in the rest of the function later in this chapter.

```
CREATE OR REPLACE PACKAGE BODY pkg_apress_plugins as

    FUNCTION f_render_from_to_datepicker (...

    FUNCTION f_validate_from_to_datepicker (...

    FUNCTION f_render_dialog (
        p_dynamic_action IN apex_plugin.t_dynamic_action,
        p_plugin         IN apex_plugin.t_plugin )
        RETURN apex_plugin.t_dynamic_action_render_result
    AS
        -- Return
        v_result apex_plugin.t_dynamic_action_render_result;

    BEGIN

        -- RETURN
        v_result;

        RETURN v_result;

    END f_render_dialog;

END pkg_apress_plugins;
/
```

Figure 4-23.pkg_apress_plugins.f_render_dialogpackage body (minimal)

The next thing to do is to modify Page 20 so that you can test the plug-in as you develop it. The following steps will remove some of the unnecessary things from Page 20 and create the necessary test items.

1. Edit Page 20, and delete the Test dynamic action.

2. Delete the TRIGGER_DYNAMIC_ACTION button.

3. Create a new HTML region with the following configuration:

Title: My Form
Sequence: 20

All other options should be left to the default settings. In the My Form region, create the following items, button, and page branch:

a. Create three Text Field page items in the My Form region called
    P20_A, P20_B, and P20_C.

b. Create a region button called Submit in the My Form region
    using the default configurations. Set its position in the bottom
    left of the region.

c. Create a page branch (On Submit: After Processing,After
    Computation, Validation, and Processing)that branches back to
    Page 20. On the Branch Conditions page, set the When Button
    Pressed field to SUBMIT (submit).

d. If you run Page 20 now, it should look like Figure 4-24.

Figure 4-24. Page 20 with three items

4. Create a new Report (Classic Report) region with the following
    configurations:

    Title: Employee Report
    Sequence: 30
    Query: SELECT * FROM emp
    Rows per Page: 5

5. If you run Page 20 now, it should look like Figure 4-25.

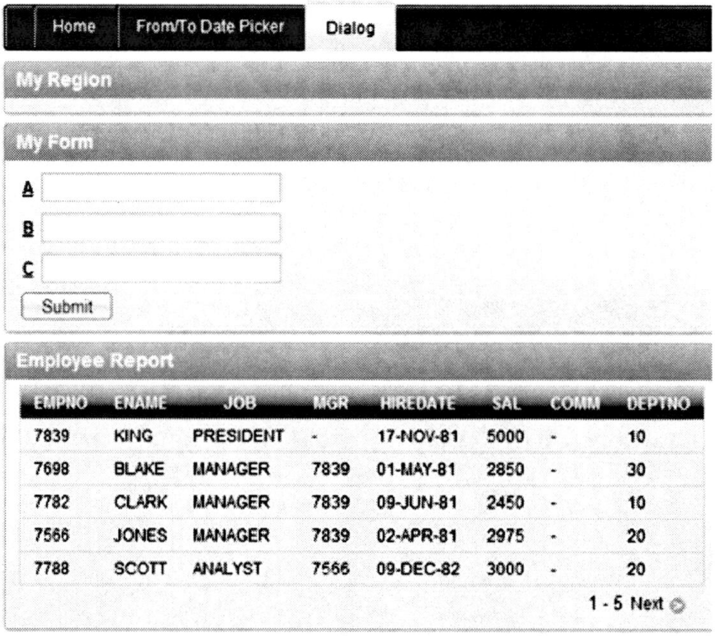

Figure 4-25. Page 20 with report

6. You will add the buttons to trigger the dynamic actions after setting up the custom attributes, so that you can see how the custom attributes are displayed in the Dynamic Action Creation wizard.

Custom Attributes

Just like the From/To Date picker item plug-in, this plug-in requires some custom attributes. Both application- and component-level attributes are necessary.

The following list describes the attributes that are required for the plug-in given the set of requirements. Create each of the following attributes using the same process as described in the preceding chapter. Refer back to that chapter if you need to refresh your memory on the process.

- *Scope*: Application
  Attribute: 1
  Label: Background Color
  Type: Text
  Required: No
  Display Width: 10

  This value is not required since it will use the default jQuery UI theme color that is defined with the APEX theme.

- *Scope*: Application
  Attribute: 2
  Label: Background Opacity
  Type: Select List
  Required: Yes
  Default: 0.3
  LOVs:

  a. *Display Value*: 10%
     Return Value: 0.1

  b. *Display Value*: 20%
     Return Value: 0.2

  c. … 30%~90%

  d. *Display Value*: 100%
     Return Value: 1

- *Scope*: Component
  Attribute: 1
  Label: Modal
  Type: Yes/No
  Default: Y

  The Yes/No value is a special type of select list that will return either Y or N. Since there are only two possible values, there is no required field. If no value is entered for the Default Value, N will be used.

- *Scope*: Component
  Attribute: 2
  Label: Close on Escape
  Type: Yes/No
  Default: Y

- *Scope*: Component
  Attribute: 3
  Label: Dialog Title
  Type: Text
  Required: No
  Translatable: Yes

  If the Translatable option is set to Yes, the value of the attribute will be included in the list of phrases to translate in multi-language applications.

- *Scope*: Component
  Attribute: 4
  Label: Hide Affected Elements on Page Load
  Type: Yes/No
  Default: Y

- *Scope*: Component
  Attribute: 5
  Label: On Close Visible State
  Type: Select List
  Required: Yes
  Default: prev
  LOVs:

  Display Value: Previous (default)
  Return Value: prev

  Display Value: Show
  Return Value: show

  Display Value: Hide
  Return Value: hide

To confirm your changes, modify the plug-in and go to the Settings region. Figure 4-26shows the two application-level attributes that are now available. Figure 4-27 shows the entire list of custom attributes for this plug-in.

Figure 4-26. Custom application attributes

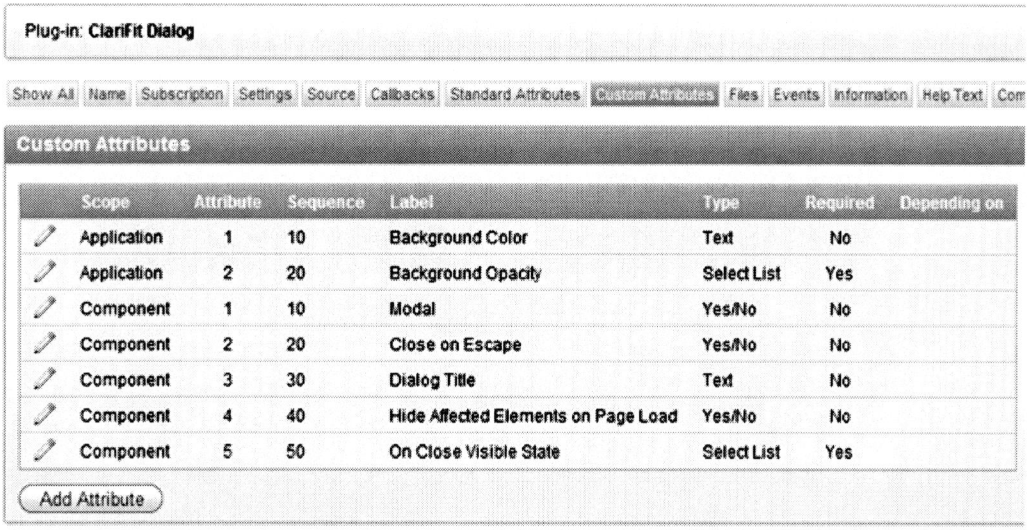

Plug-in: ClariFit Dialog

Show All | Name | Subscription | Settings | Source | Callbacks | Standard Attributes | Custom Attributes | Files | Events | Information | Help Text | Com

Custom Attributes

	Scope	Attribute	Sequence	Label	Type	Required	Depending on
✎	Application	1	10	Background Color	Text	No	
✎	Application	2	20	Background Opacity	Select List	Yes	
✎	Component	1	10	Modal	Yes/No	No	
✎	Component	2	20	Close on Escape	Yes/No	No	
✎	Component	3	30	Dialog Title	Text	No	
✎	Component	4	40	Hide Affected Elements on Page Load	Yes/No	No	
✎	Component	5	50	On Close Visible State	Select List	Yes	

(Add Attribute)

Figure 4-27. Dialog plug-in custom attributes

If you encountered any issues creating the custom attributes, please refer to the sample application that comes with this book. The help text was excluded from the foregoing descriptions, but they are included in the sample applications.

Now that the custom attributes have been defined, when you use this plug-in in a dynamic action, you will see the component-level custom attributes in the Settings page (wizard) or Settings region. The following steps create two buttons that leverage this dynamic action plug-in:

1. Edit Page 20. Create a region button called Dialog My Form. On the Action When Clicked page, set the Action field to Defined by Dynamic Action, as shown in Figure 4-1.

2. Create another button with the same attributes, but change its name to Dialog Emp Report. This button will be used to trigger the dialog window for the Employee Report region.

3. Run Page 20. It should now look like Figure 4-28. Note that the buttons'
    positions have been set to the bottom left of the region to help with the
    screenshots in this book. If you used the default option, they will be in the
    top right corner of the My Region region.

    If you click either of the buttons, nothing happens, as there are no
    dynamic actions registered to them. This will be done in the next step.

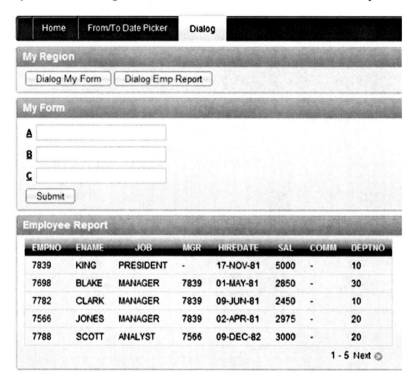

Figure 4-28. Buttons added to My Region

4. Create a dynamic action on the DIALOG_MY_FORMbutton. Here are the
    steps to follow:

a. Edit Page 20. Right-click the DIALOG_MY_FORM button, and select the Create Dynamic Action option from the context menu, as shown in Figure 4-29.

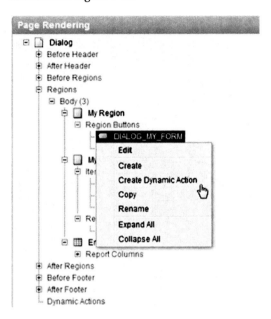

Figure 4-29. Create Dynamic Action option for DIALOG_MY_FORM button

b. On the Identification page, set the Name field to Dialog Window. Click the Next button to continue.

c. Use the default options on the When page, as shown in Figure 4-30. Click the Next button to continue.

Figure 4-30. Default When options

d. On the True Action page, set Action to ClariFit Dialog [Plug-in]. Modify the settings so that they are the same as Figure 4-31. These settings are the custom attributes that you just added to the plug-in. Click the Next button to continue.

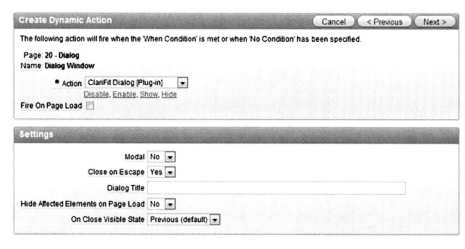

Figure 4-31. Dialog plug-in settings

e. On the Affected Elements screen, set the Selection Typefield to Region and the Regionfield to My Form(1) 20. Click the Create button to complete the wizard.

5. Create a dynamic action on the DIALOG_EMP_REPORTbutton. These steps are very similar to the previous steps with some slight modifications, and are as follows:

    a. Right-click the DIALOG_EMP_REPORT button, and select the Create Dynamic Actionoption from the context menu.

    b. On the Identification page, set the Namefield to Modal Window. Click the Next button to continue.

    c. Use the default options on the When page. Click the Next button to continue.

    d. On the True Action page, set Action to ClariFit Dialog [Plug-in]. Use the default plug-in settings, and click the Next button to continue.

    e. On the Affected Elements screen, set the Selection Typefield to Region and the Regionfield to Employee Report (1) 30. Click the Create button to complete the wizard.

f.   If you go back to the Page 20 edit page, it should look like Figure
4-32. In Figure 4-32, the tree elements for the buttons have been
expanded to show all the dynamic action information.

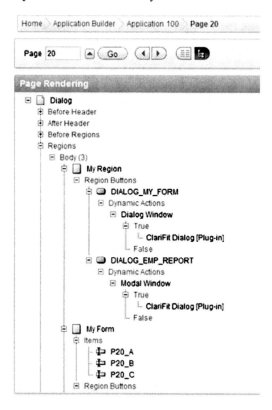

Figure 4-32. Page 20 dynamic actions

If you run Page 20, it will load but the buttons won't do anything, as the PL/SQL code is not
complete nor is there any JavaScript code. You may also notice some JavaScript errors when the page
loads. These errors will go away when you finish coding the render function and the JavaScript code.

Render Function

Now that everything is set up, there are two key pieces missing for this dynamic action plug-in: the
PL/SQL render function and the JavaScript code. This section will display all the PL/SQL code and give a
full analysis based on the line numbers. The line numbers don't start at 1 since there's code from a
previous plug-in in this chapter.

■ **Note** In the previous chapter, the JavaScript section was before the PL/SQL render function, whereas this chapter covers the render function first and then the JavaScript code. Developing a plug-in usually involves an iterative approach. Once you get the base functionality working, you will probably work with both sets of code at the same time.

Copy the following code (excluding the line numbers) into the package body for pks_apress_plugins. An analysis of the code follows.

```
227 ...
228
229 FUNCTION f_render_dialog (
230   p_dynamic_action IN apex_plugin.t_dynamic_action,
231   p_plugin         IN apex_plugin.t_plugin )
232   RETURN apex_plugin.t_dynamic_action_render_result
233 AS
234   -- Application Plugin Attributes
235   v_background_color apex_appl_plugins.attribute_01%TYPE := p_plugin.attribute_01;
236   v_background_opacity apex_appl_plugins.attribute_01%TYPE := p_plugin.attribute_02;
237
238   -- DA Plugin Attributes
239   v_modal apex_application_page_items.attribute_01%TYPE := p_dynamic_action.attribute_01;
-- y/n
240   v_close_on_esc apex_application_page_items.attribute_01%TYPE :=
p_dynamic_action.attribute_02; -- y/n
241   v_title apex_application_page_items.attribute_01%TYPE := p_dynamic_action.attribute_03;
-- text
242   v_hide_on_load apex_application_page_items.attribute_01%TYPE :=
upper(p_dynamic_action.attribute_04); -- y/n
243   v_on_close_visible_state apex_application_page_items.attribute_01%type :=
lower(p_dynamic_action.attribute_05); -- prev, show, hide
244
245   -- Return
246   v_result apex_plugin.t_dynamic_action_render_result;
247
248   -- Other variables
249   v_html varchar2(4000);
250   v_affected_elements apex_application_page_da_acts.affected_elements%type;
251   v_affected_elements_type apex_application_page_da_acts.affected_elements_type%type;
252   v_affected_region_id apex_application_page_da_acts.affected_region_id%type;
253   v_affected_region_static_id apex_application_page_regions.static_id%type;
254
255   -- Convert Y/N to True/False (text)
256   -- Default to true
257   FUNCTION f_yn_to_true_false_str(p_val IN VARCHAR2)
258   RETURN VARCHAR2
259   AS
260   BEGIN
```

```
261    RETURN
262      CASE
263        WHEN p_val IS NULL OR lower(p_val) != 'n' THEN 'true'
264        ELSE 'false'
265      END;
266   END f_yn_to_true_false_str;
267
268 BEGIN
269   -- Debug information (if app is being run in debug mode)
270   IF apex_application.g_debug THEN
271     apex_plugin_util.debug_dynamic_action (
272       p_plugin => p_plugin,
273       p_dynamic_action => p_dynamic_action);
274   END IF;
275
276   -- Cleanup values
277   v_modal := f_yn_to_true_false_str(p_val => v_modal);
278   v_close_on_esc := f_yn_to_true_false_str(p_val => v_close_on_esc);
279
280   -- If Background color is not null set the CSS
281   -- This will be done only once per page
282   IF v_background_color IS NOT NULL THEN
283     v_html := q'!
284       .ui-widget-overlay{
285         background-image: none ;
286         background-color: %BG_COLOR%;
287         opacity: %OPACITY%;
288       }!';
289
290     v_html := REPLACE(v_html, '%BG_COLOR%', v_background_color);
291     v_html := REPLACE(v_html, '%OPACITY%', v_background_opacitiy);
292
293     apex_css.ADD (
294       p_css => v_html,
295       p_key => 'ui.clarifitdialog.background');
296   END IF;
297
298   -- JAVASCRIPT
299
300   -- Load javascript Libraries
301   apex_javascript.add_library (p_name => '$console_wrapper', p_directory =>
p_plugin.file_prefix, p_version=> '_1.0.3'); -- Load Console Wrapper for debugging
302   apex_javascript.add_library (p_name => 'jquery.ui.clarifitDialog', p_directory =>
p_plugin.file_prefix, p_version=> '_1.0.0');
303
304   -- Hide Affected Elements on Load
305   IF v_hide_on_load = 'Y' THEN
306
307     v_html := '';
308
309     SELECT affected_elements, lower(affected_elements_type), affected_region_id,
aapr.static_id
```

```
310     INTO v_affected_elements, v_affected_elements_type, v_affected_region_id,
v_affected_region_static_id
311     FROM apex_application_page_da_acts aapda, apex_application_page_regions aapr
312     WHERE aapda.action_id = p_dynamic_action.ID
313       AND aapda.affected_region_id = aapr.region_id(+);
314
315     IF v_affected_elements_type = 'jquery selector' THEN
316       v_html := 'apex.jQuery("' || v_affected_elements || '").hide();';
317     ELSIF v_affected_elements_type = 'dom object' THEN
318       v_html := 'apex.jQuery("#' || v_affected_elements || '").hide();';
319     ELSIF v_affected_elements_type = 'region' THEN
320       v_html := 'apex.jQuery("#' || nvl(v_affected_region_static_id, 'R' ||
v_affected_region_id) || '").hide();';
321     ELSE
322       -- unknown/unhandled (nothing to hide)
323       raise_application_error(-20001, 'Unknown Affected Element Type');
324     END IF; -- v_affected_elements_type
325
326     apex_javascript.add_onload_code (
327       p_code => v_html,
328       p_key  => NULL); -- Leave null so always run
329   END IF; -- v_hide_on_load
330
331   -- RETURN
332   v_result.javascript_function := '$.ui.clarifitDialog.daDialog';
333   v_result.attribute_01 := v_modal;
334   v_result.attribute_02 := v_close_on_esc;
335   v_result.attribute_03 := v_title;
336   v_result.attribute_04 := v_on_close_visible_state;
337
338   RETURN v_result;
339
340 END f_render_dialog;
341
342 ...
```

Here is an explanation of key passages in the preceding code listing:

234–243: Application- and component-level custom attributes; remember to use meaningful names to describe them rather than their attribute number. It may also be helpful to put a comment on expected values when applicable so that other developers know what values to expect.

250–253: Variables to store the affected elements; generally, in dynamic action plug-ins, this information is required only in the JavaScript code (which can be referenced in the `this` object). Due to the requirement of hiding the object on page load, the affected element is required here. This will be discussed further in the code analysis.

257–266: Inline function to convert Y/N values to true/false (string) values; this is not required, but if you need to convert some of the same types, attributes creating inline functions can save time.

270–274: Standard debugging code; you can instrument the rest of your function with more debugging code but at a minimum including this debug statement.

280–296: This code sets the background color and opacity for modal windows. This is a page-level setting (i.e., will be the same for all the modal windows).

You could use `htp.p` to output the code; however, it would be run for each instance of this plug-in. In the example, it would be run twice because there aretwo instances of the same plug-in on the page. Since it needs to be run only once, there's a parameter called `p_key` (line 295). If this key has already been used, the code will not be reprinted. If the key is null, it will always be used.

300–302: Load JavaScript files.

304–329: This is a unique block of code. One of the custom attributes allows an APEX developer to hide the affected region on page load. Since the dynamic action code is run only when it is triggered, additional steps are required to find the affected elements and explicitly hide them once the page is loaded.

On lines **316, 318,** and **320**, the JavaScript references the `apex.jQuery`namespace rather than $. This ensures that it is actually referencing the jQuery code rather than a different JavaScript library.

On line **328**,`p_key` is set to `NULL` (default value). This means that the code will always be run. Since `NULL` is the default value, you don't need to explicitly reference it if you don't need it.

331–336: Defines the return object; the first thing you'll notice is that there's no explicit call to actually "run" any JavaScript code to trigger your plug-in like an item plug-in. Instead, all you need to do is define the JavaScript function name. This function should not take in any parameters, as all the values that you need are available in the dynamic action `this` object (discussed earlier in this chapter).

Lines **333–336** set attributes that are available in the `this.action`JavaScript object. These attributes are *not*the same as custom (application and component) attributes. These attributes are passed as strings, so you should ensure that you convert any non-string values to strings when setting them. This is why the Y/N values (`v_modal` and `v_close_on_esc`) are converted to string true/false values rather than Oracle Boolean values.

JavaScript

Similar to the previous section, this section will list the JavaScript code and then break down each section. Before continuing, you'll need to download and copy `$console_wrapper_1.0.3.js` and `jquery.ui.clarifitDialog_1.0.0.js`into `c:\www\ApexDialog` (or the appropriate web server directory) for this plug-in to work. These files are available in the source code files that accompany this book.Since the previous chapter covered how to embed JavaScript files directly into your plug-in, this chapter will not do so. You are encouraged to review the previous chapter (see the "Wrapping Up" section) and embed the JavaScript files on your own.

Here is a complete listing of **jquery.ui.clarifitDialog_1.0.0.js** followed by a breakdown of each section. When reading through this code, you should start to notice how everything nicely meshes together.

```
001 /**
002  * ClariFit jQuery UI Dialog
003  * Plug-in Type: Dynamic Action
004  * Summary: Displays a jQuery UI Dialog window for affected elements
005  *
006  * Depends:
007  *   jquery.ui.dialog.js
008  *   $.console.js  - http://code.google.com/p/js-console-wrapper/
009  *
010  * Notes:
011  * Object to be shown in Dialog window needs to be wrapped in order to preserve its
position in DOM
012  * See: http://forums.oracle.com/forums/thread.jspa?messageID=3180532 for more
information.
013  *
014  * ^^^ Contact information ^^^
015  * Developed by ClariFit Inc.
016  * http://www.clarifit.com
017  * apex@clarifit.com
018  *
019  * ^^^ License ^^^
020  * Licensed Under: GNU General Public License, version 3 (GPL-3.0) -
www.opensource.org/licenses/gpl-3.0.html
021  *
022  * @author Martin Giffy D'Souza - www.talkapex.com
023  */
024 (function($){
025 $.widget('ui.clarifitDialog', {
026   // default options
027   options: {
028     //Configurable options in APEX plugin
029     modal: true,
030     closeOnEscape: true,
031     title: '',
032     persist: true, //Future option, no affect right now
033     onCloseVisibleState: 'prev' //Restore objects visible state once closed
034   },
035
036   /**
037    * Init function. This function will be called each time the widget is referenced with
no parameters
038    */
039   _init: function(){
040     var uiw = this;
041     var consoleGroupName = uiw._scope + '._init';
042     $.console.groupCollapsed(consoleGroupName);
043
```

```
044      //Find the objects visible state before making dialog window (used to restore if
necessary)
045      uiw._values.beforeShowVisible = uiw._elements.$element.is(':visible');
046      $.console.log('beforeShowVisible: ', uiw._values.beforeShowVisible);
047
048      //Create Dialog window
049      //Creating each time so that we can easily restore its visible state if necessary
050      uiw._elements.$element.dialog({
051        modal: uiw.options.modal,
052        closeOnEscape: uiw.options.closeOnEscape,
053        title: uiw.options.title,
054        //Options below Can be made configurable if required
055        width: 'auto',
056        //Event Binding
057        beforeClose: function(event, ui) {  $(this).trigger('cfpluginapexdialogbeforeclose',
{event: event, ui: ui}); },
058        close: function(event, ui) {
059          //Destroy the jQuery UI elements so that it displays as if dialog had not been
applied
060          uiw._elements.$element.dialog( "destroy" );
061
062          //Move out of wrapper and back into original position
063          uiw._elements.$wrapper.before(uiw._elements.$element);
064
065          //Show only if previous state was show
066          if ((uiw._values.beforeShowVisible && uiw.options.onCloseVisibleState == 'prev')
|| uiw.options.onCloseVisibleState == 'show'){
067              uiw._elements.$element.show();
068          }
069          else {
070              uiw._elements.$element.hide();
071          }
072
073          //Trigger custom APEX Event
074          uiw._elements.$element.trigger('cfpluginapexdialogclose', {event: event, ui: ui});
075        },
076        create: function(event, ui) {  $(this).trigger('cfpluginapexdialogcreate', {event:
event, ui: ui}); }
077      });
078
079      //Move into wrapper
080      uiw._elements.$wrapper.append(uiw._elements.$element.parent('.ui-dialog'));
081
082      $.console.groupEnd(consoleGroupName);
083    }, //_init
084
085    /**
086     * Set private widget variables
087     */
088    _setWidgetVars: function(){
089      var uiw = this;
090
```

```
091     uiw._scope = 'ui.' + uiw.widgetName; //For debugging
092
093     uiw._values = {
094        wrapperId : uiw.widgetName + '_' + parseInt(Math.random()*10000000000000000),
//Random number to identify wrapper
095        beforeShowVisible: false //Visible state before show
096     };
097
098     uiw._elements = {
099        $element : $(uiw.element[0]), //Affected element
100        $wrapper : null
101     };
102
103   }, //_setWidgetVars
104
105   /**
106    * Create function: Called the first time widget is associated to the object
107    * Does all the required setup, etc. and binds change event
108    */
109   _create: function(){
110     var uiw = this;
111
112     uiw._setWidgetVars();
113
114     var consoleGroupName = uiw._scope + '._create';
115     $.console.groupCollapsed(consoleGroupName);
116     $.console.log('this:', uiw);
117     $.console.log('element:', uiw.element[0]);
118
119     //Create wrapper so that we keep object in its current place on the DOM
120     uiw._elements.$element.wrap('<div id="' + uiw._values.wrapperId + '"/>');
121     uiw._elements.$wrapper = $('#' + uiw._values.wrapperId);
122     $.console.log('wrapperId: ', uiw._values.wrapperId);
123
124     $.console.groupEnd(consoleGroupName);
125   },//_create
126
127   /**
128    * Removes all functionality associated with the clarifitDialog
129    * Will remove the change event as well
130    * Odds are this will not be called from APEX.
131    */
132   destroy: function() {
133     var uiw = this;
134
135     $.console.log(uiw._scope, 'destroy', uiw);
136     $.Widget.prototype.destroy.apply(uiw, arguments); // default destroy
137     // unregister datepicker
138     uiw._elements.$element.dialog( "destroy" )
139   }//destroy
140 }); //ui.clarifitDialog
141
```

```
142 $.extend($.ui.clarifitDialog, {
143    /**
144     * Function to be called from the APEX Dynamic Action process
145     * No values are passed in
146     * "this" is the APEX DA "this" object
147     */
148    daDialog: function(){
149       var scope = '$.ui.clarifitDialog.daDialog';
150       var daThis = this; //Note that "this" represents the APEX Dynamic Action object
151       $.console.groupCollapsed(scope);
152       $.console.log('APEX DA this: ' , daThis);
153
154       //Set options
155       var options = {
156          modal: daThis.action.attribute01 === 'false' ?false : true,
157          closeOnEscape: daThis.action.attribute02 === 'false' ?false : true,
158          title: daThis.action.attribute03,
159          onCloseVisibleState: daThis.action.attribute04
160       };
161
162       for(var i = 0, end = daThis.affectedElements.length; i < end; i++){
163          $.console.log('Dialoging: ', daThis.affectedElements[i]);
164          $(daThis.affectedElements[i]).clarifitDialog(options);
165       }//for
166
167       $.console.groupEnd(scope);
168    }//daDialog
169
170 });//Extend
171
172 })(apex.jQuery);
```

Here is an explanation of key passages in the preceding JavaScript code listing:

001–023: Plug-in comment and license information; always spend the extra few minutes and include some notes about the code. You'll be thankful in the long run.

024+172: Namespacing the jQuery variable name, which was discussed in the previous chapter; if you do not use this technique, you should reference apex.jQuery instead of $.

025–140: jQuery UI Widget Factory code for this plug-in

033: onCloseVisibleState defines what to do with the dialog window once it's closed. This code supports it going back to its previous state (default option), always showing, or always hiding.

050–077: Display the dialog window; stores the visible state of the object before it is converted to a dialog window. This is necessary to restore the window as defined by one of the plug-in's custom attributes.

This code also supports custom event binding. For example, line **057** will trigger a custom event, which other APEX dynamic actions can leverage. This is defined in the Events region in the plug-in.

On line **080**, the element is moved into a wrapper. This is to ensure that the page items remain in the same order that they were loaded on the page. For more information, see the forum posting at the beginning of the file.

085–103: Set private variables for the widget; note that, though they appear to be private variables, if end users really wanted to modify them, they could.

105–140: Create function that creates a wrapper for the affected element; the _initfunctionrequires the wrapper to protect the order of the object in the DOM.

142–170: This is static code that acts as the middle man between the call from APEX and the UI Widget. `daDialog` does not require any parameters since it obtains all the necessary information from the `this` object.

The variable `daThis` refers to the dynamic action `this` variable, which contains everything about the dynamic action.

Lines **156–159** reference the dynamic action attributes. Again, these are *not* the same as the plug-in's custom attributes. They are defined in the returned PL/SQL object.

Since the dynamic actions attributes are passed as strings, they need to be explicitly converted to JavaScript objects (when applicable). Lines **156–157** convert attributes from strings to JavaScript Booleans.

Line **162** references the `affectedElements` to apply the JavaScript code to. The JavaScript code does not necessarily care if the affected element(s) is a region or a jQuery Selector, etc. APEX gives it an array of objects to work with.

Testing It Out

Since you have completed all the code and configuration, and built a good test page, it's time to test your plug-in. To start, refresh Page 20. It should look like Figure 4-33. The most noticeable difference is that the Employee report is hidden since it was one of the plug-in's configuration options.

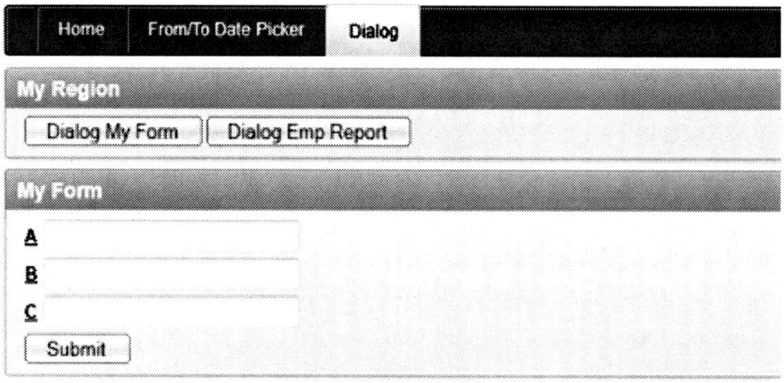

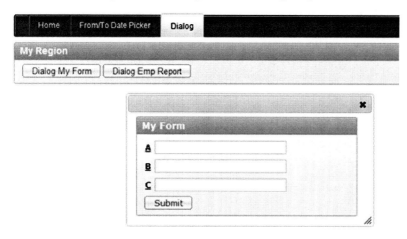

Figure 4-33. Page 20 final

If you click the Dialog My Form button, the My Form region now becomes a dialog window, as shown in Figure 4-34. Since it is not a modal window, you can click outside of the dialog window. When you close the dialog window, it will go back to its original position and visibility state.

Figure 4-34. My Form dialog window

If you click the Dialog Emp Report button, the Employee Report region will appear as a modal window, like Figure 4-35. When you close the modal window, it will disappear.

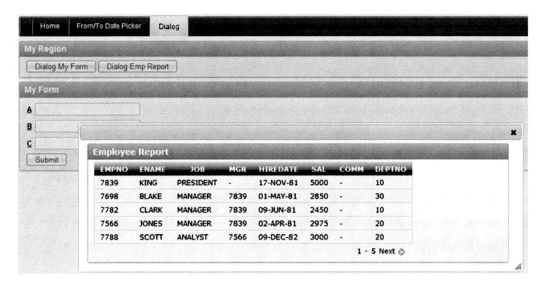

Figure 4-35. Employee Report modal window

You are encouraged to modify each of the dynamic actions plug-in settings to see how they affect the outcome.

Summary

This chapter covered what dynamic actions are and how they work. Dynamic actions declaratively let APEX developers define and implement front-end events.

Compared to items, dynamic actions can be a bit more complex, which can make them difficult to understand. It is important to have a solid understanding of their internal mechanisms before developing a plug-in.

You may also start to notice some similarities between dynamic action and item plug-ins, such as the render function, JavaScript code, and custom attributes. Having these similarities helps when you are learning the APEX plug-in architecture.

CHAPTER 5

■ ■ ■

Region Plug-Ins

Region plug-ins, as you may guess, allow you to create your own region types in APEX. Before APEX 4.0, if you wanted to create a "custom" region you would need to create a PL/SQL type region that would generate all the content for your custom region. Region plug-ins take a similar approach, and also provide an excellent declarative and supported framework for managing custom region types.

This chapter explains what region plug-ins do and don't cover, helps you build a region plug-in, and introduces AJAX functionalities. The plug-ins covered in previous chapters (item and dynamic action) also support AJAX functionality, so the AJAX content in this chapter is relevant to the previous two plug-in types as well.

Background on Regions and AJAX

Before developing a region plug-in with AJAX support, it's important to cover two things: the architecture of a region (i.e., the difference between the region itself and a region template) and AJAX in APEX. It is important to understand these topics before developing the region plug-in and adding in AJAX functionality.

Regions

The easiest way to explain the architecture of a region is by analyzing one. Figure 5-1 shows the *My Form* region that you created in the previous chapter. The content inside the dotted line is part of the region's body. The content outside the dotted line is part of the region template. Region plug-ins only generate content for the region body and they don't need to be concerned with the region template. The region template will wrap the region body with the standard display code, which is determined by the APEX developer.

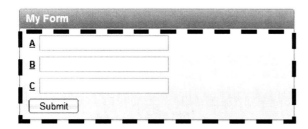

Figure 5-1. Region body outline

Another way to view the difference between the region content and the template is to examine the region template. Region templates define the look and feel of the region. To view the region template

1. Go to the application's Shared Components.

2. Under the User Interface, click on the **Templates** link as shown in Figure 5-2.

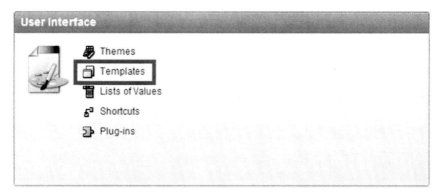

Figure 5-2. Templates link in Shared Components

3. Filter the templates report by setting the *Type* list to **Region**.

4. Click on the default region. The default region has a check mark in the *Default* column. Figure 5-3 shows the default region template in the application as Reports Region.

Report Filter - Single Row	0	-	-	-	-	1		
Reports Region	6	-	-	-	✓	1		
Reports Region 100% Width	0	-	-	-	-	1		

Figure 5-3. Default region template

5. On the Edit Region Template page, scroll down to the Definition region. Figure 5-4 shows the content of the Template text area.

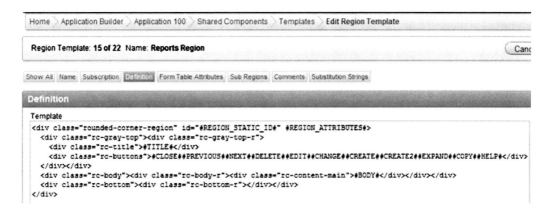

Figure 5-4. Region template definition

In Figure 5-4, you'll notice that there are some HTML tags that wrap the content of the region. These are some special tags that APEX will replace with the appropriate region attributes such as *#TITLE#* and the button tags (*#CLOSE#*, *#PREVIOUS#*, … ,*#HELP#*). The *#BODY#* substitution string is what will be replaced with the content from the region plug-in.

Because the region plug-in handles only the "meat" of the region, region plug-ins need only to focus on what is necessary to be displayed as part of the region. You don't need to be concerned about styling the region, displaying the region buttons, and so on, since the region template handles all these elements.

AJAX

At a very high level, AJAX allows the browser to send data to the server and receive a response back from it without having to submit the page. With respect to APEX, this means that you can send some data to APEX, run a block of PL/SQL code, and send data back to the browser without having to submit the page.

■ **Note** Wikipedia has an excellent description of AJAX at the following link:

http://en.wikipedia.org/wiki/Ajax_(programming).

Prior to APEX 4.0, AJAX functions were handled through an On Demand application process. Though it is not required, building an AJAX function using the old (pre-APEX 4.0) method may help you understand and appreciate how the new plug-in AJAX function works. The following steps cover how to build and use a simple AJAX function the "old way." This function will send the user's current value to APEX and return the value multiplied by two.

■ **Note** With APEX 4.0, manually creating AJAX functions is not required because the same functionality can easily be provided by a dynamic action of type PL/SQL. This example is solely to demonstrate how things work and is not a recommended practice for making AJAX calls in APEX 4.0 and higher.

1. Create a new blank page with the following attributes:

   Page Number: **30**
   Name: **AJAX (Old)**
   HTML Region 1: **My Region**
   Tab: **AJAX (Old)**

2. Edit the new page, Page 30, and create a new page item in *My Region* with the following attributes:

   Item Type: **Number Field**
   Item Name: **P30_X**

3. Create a region button with the following attributes:

   Button Name: **Run AJAX**
   Button Alignment: **Left**
   Action: **Defined by Dynamic Action**

   If you run Page 30, it should now look like Figure 5-5.

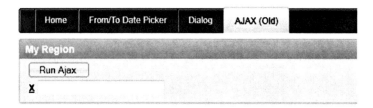

Figure 5-5. AJAX demo page

4. Go to Shared Components and click on the **Application Processes** link as shown in Figure 5-6.

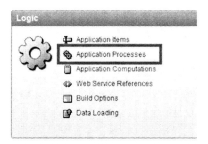

Figure 5-6. Application Processes link in Shared Components

5. In the Application Processes window, click the Create button.

6. On the Identification wizard page, enter the values as shown in Figure 5-7. Setting the *Point* to **On Demand…** allows this process to be accessible via an AJAX call. Click the Next button to go to the next step.

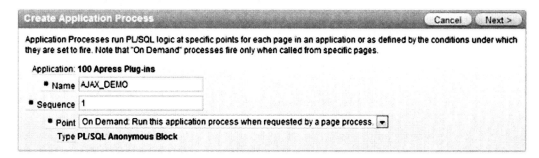

Figure 5-7. Create Application Process > Identification

7. On the Source page, enter the following PL/SQL code in the *Process Text* text area. This is the code that will be run when the AJAX function is triggered by the browser. Click the Next button to continue.

In the code, `apex_application.g_x01` is a value that will be passed from the AJAX JavaScript call to APEX. APEX supports up to ten values (`apex_application.g_x01 .. apex_application.g_x10`) along with one clob value (`apex_application.g_clob_01`).

The PL/SQL code "sends" a value back to the client's browser by printing the value with the `htp.p` call. JavaScript will interpret this value as a string that will need to be converted accordingly.

```
-- Takes value and multiplies it by 2
-- No error handling etc, as this is a demo
DECLARE
```

```
  v_num pls_integer;
BEGIN
  v_num := to_number(apex_application.g_x01);

  v_num := v_num * 2;

  htp.p (v_num);
END;
```

8. On the Conditionality page, leave the default options (i.e., no condition) and click the Create Process to complete the wizard.

9. The final thing to do is to write the JavaScript code that will trigger the AJAX call. Edit Page 30 and right click on the *RUN_AJAX* button. Select the **Create Dynamic Action** option from the context menu.

10. In the Identification section, set the *Name* to **Run AJAX Function**. Click the Next button to continue.

11. Figure 5-8 shows the default options on the When page. Leave these settings and click the Next button.

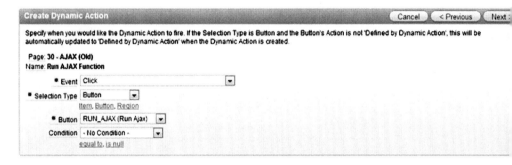

Figure 5-8. Create Dynamic Action > When

12. On the True Action page, set the *Action* to **Execute JavaScript Code**. **Uncheck** the *Fire On Page Load* check box. Enter the following JavaScript code in the *Code* text area. Click the Next button to continue.

In the JavaScript code below, you'll notice that the first line of code references the *AJAX_DEMO* application process.

The function addParam defines the x01..x10 values that will set the PL/SQL apex_application.g_x01 .. apex_application.g_x10 variables as part of the AJAX request.

```
// Demo code for AJAX calls
var ajax = new htmldb_Get(null,$v('pFlowId'), 'APPLICATION_PROCESS=AJAX_DEMO',0);

// Value to send to PL/SQL code
// Note: this does not "submit" P30_X (that can be done but in another way)
ajax.addParam('x01', $v('P30_X'));
```

```
// Trigger AJAX call (will send POST to APEX)
var ajaxResult = ajax.get();

// Display the result in an alert window
window.alert(ajaxResult);
```

    a.

    b.

13. On the Affected Elements page, click the Create button to finish the wizard.

14. Run Page 30. Enter **2** in the text box and click the **Run Ajax** button. An alert window should pop up with the value *4*, as shown in Figure 5-9.

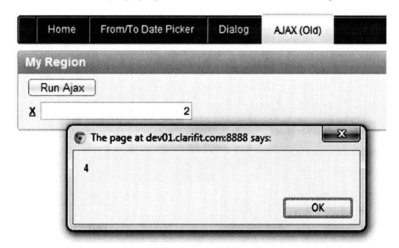

Figure 5-9. Run AJAX result

▦ **Note** `apex_application.g_x01..x10` variables are not associated with `plugin.attribute_01..15` variables. They are submitted as part of every APEX request and a globally accessible (i.e., they're not specific to any particular object).

If you open the Console window, you'll see the POST request that the browser made to the server. Figure 5-10 shows the result from the POST request. From the console result, you can clearly see how the values are sent to the server. Figure 5-11 shows the response back from the server. As previously mentioned, this result is a simple string in JavaScript. If you need to do anything with it, you'll need to explicitly convert it to the correct data type. In this example, you'd need to convert it to a number.

Implementing AJAX functionality via a plug-in is much easier to do than the process just described. In the region plug-in example to follow, you will create an AJAX function and you should be able to see the common features with this example.

Figure 5-10. AJAX POST request

Figure 5-11. AJAX POST response

Example Business Problem

As with the other plug-ins, the first thing you should do is state your business requirements. This region plug-in should display the titles from an RSS feed. The plug-in should also implement some additional related functionality. The following is the complete list of requirements:

- Display a list of RSS feed titles.

- Configure the maximum number of RSS feeds in the region, ranging from 5, 10, and 15 items.

- Needs to currently support RSS feeds from Blogger (`www.blogger.com`).

- When a user clicks on an RSS title, a modal window appears and displays the content of the RSS feed. The default modal window size will be configurable.

The plug-in you are going to build will use some of the UTL_HTTP features in Oracle to obtain RSS feeds. HTTP access and other network services are potential security vulnerabilities, so their access is restricted in Oracle Database 11g and higher. You will need to enable network services and grant access to them in order to create the plug-in described next.

■ **Note** If running Oracle Database 10g or lower, you can skip this section. HTTP access is not restricted in those lower releases. If you are using apex.oracle.com as your server, then you won't be able to create this chapter's plug-in at all. That's because apex.oracle.com restricts UTL_HTTP access.

Think twice about enabling UTL_HTTP access in a production environment. Discuss such changes with your database administrator. Be sure that you do not violate any security policies. The example to follow is meant for demonstration purposes and should be thoroughly reviewed before implementation in a production environment.

The following are the assumptions made in describing the process of enabling the UTL_HTTP access needed by this chapter's example plug-in:

- The current user that the APEX application is being run as (i.e., parsing schema) is the *APRESS* user. In the scripts and queries below, substitute *APRESS* for your user.

- Unless explicitly specified, scripts and queries will be run as the *SYSTEM* or *SYS* user. You may need to ask your DBA to run these scripts for you.

All the scripts are in the files included with this book. If your environment is not as described in the preceding list, you will need to modify the scripts before executing them. For example, you may need to substitute in the user name that you are using.

When you have the scripts ready for your environment, follow these steps to enable UTL_HTTP access:

1. Run the following, which will grant access to external networks for your current user. Don't forget to change the value of **v_user** to your username.

```
-- Run as SYSTEM or SYS
-- Creates a ACL with access to all domains and ports
-- Or leverages one that already exists
DECLARE
  v_acl dba_network_acls.acl%TYPE;
  v_user VARCHAR2(30) := 'APRESS'; -- *** CHANGE TO YOUR USER
  v_cnt pls_integer;
BEGIN
  v_user := upper(v_user);

  -- Get current ACL (if it exists)
  SELECT max(acl)
  INTO v_acl
  FROM dba_network_acls
  WHERE host = '*'
    AND lower_port IS NULL
    AND upper_port IS NULL;
```

```
    IF v_acl IS NULL THEN
      -- No ACL exists. Create one
      v_acl := 'apress_full_access.xml';

      -- Create ACL with access to your user
      dbms_network_acl_admin.create_acl (
        acl         => v_acl,
        description => 'ACL Access for Apress demo',
        principal   => v_user,
        is_grant    => TRUE,
        privilege   => 'connect',
        start_date  => NULL,
        end_date    => NULL);

      -- Grant access to ACL to all ports and ports
      dbms_network_acl_admin.assign_acl (
        acl         => v_acl,
        host        => '*', -- This is the network that you have access to.
        lower_port  => NULL,
        upper_port  => NULL);
    ELSE
      -- ACL Exists, just need to give access to user (if applicable)
      SELECT count(acl)
      INTO v_cnt
      FROM dba_network_acl_privileges
      WHERE acl = v_acl
        and principal = v_user;

      IF v_cnt = 0 THEN
        -- User needs to be granted
        dbms_network_acl_admin.add_privilege(
          acl         => v_acl,
          principal => v_user,
          is_grant  => true,
          PRIVILEGE => 'connect');
      ELSE
        -- User has access to network
        -- Nothing to be done
        NULL;
      END IF;

    END IF;

  COMMIT;

END;
/
```

2. Execute the following queries to confirm that the ACL setup worked. You should see your user associated to the network ACL with full access.

```
-- All ACLs
SELECT host, lower_port, upper_port, acl
FROM dba_network_acls;

-- Privileges for ACLs
-- Lists which users have access to which ACL
SELECT acl, principal, privilege, is_grant, invert, start_date, end_date
FROM dba_network_acl_privileges;
```

3. Confirm that your user now has network access by running the following script, with *DBMS_OUTPUT* enabled as your current user. You should see "*Ok. Have access*" as part of the output.

```
-- Test that user has network access now
-- Run as APRESS user
-- Determines if current user has access to external connections
-- Makes a simple connection to www.google.com on port 80
-- Result will be in DBMS_OUTPUT
DECLARE
  v_connection   utl_tcp.connection;
BEGIN
  v_connection := utl_tcp.open_connection(remote_host => 'www.google.com', remote_port => 80);
  utl_tcp.close_connection(v_connection);

  dbms_output.put_line('Ok: Have Access');

  EXCEPTION
    WHEN others THEN
      IF sqlcode = -24247 THEN
        -- ORA-24247: network access denied by access control list (ACL)
        dbms_output.put_line('No ACL network access.');
      ELSE
        dbms_output.put_line('Unknown Error: ' || sqlerrm);
      END IF;
END;
/
```

If you see the message "Ok. Have access," then all is well. Proceed with creating the example plug-in.

Building the Region Plug-in

Now that the business requirements have been defined, you can start creating the region plug-in. Similar to the dynamic action plug-in example in the preceding chapter, some steps will not be covered on a step-by-step basis as they have already been covered previously.

Initial Configuration and Setup

To start building a region plug-in, create a new plug-in with the attributes listed below. Once you are finished, click the Create button to save the plug-in.

Name: **ClariFit RSS Reader**

Internal Name: **COM.CLARIFIT.APEXPLUGIN.RSS_READER**

Type: **Region**

Next, create a directory to store and reference external web files. This will allow you to easily make modifications as you build your plug-in. Here are the steps:

1. Create a directory called **c:\www\RSSReader**

2. Modify the plug-in. In the Settings region set the *File Prefix* to **http://localhost/RSSReader/**

3. Click the Apply Changes button to save your changes.

Scroll down to the Standard Attributes section and check off the has **"Escape Special Characters" Attribute** option as shown in Figure 5-12. Click the Apply Changes button to save your change. In this plug-in, the *Escape Special Characters* attribute will be used to escape the RSS feed content (if enabled in region). The RSS feed URL will be defined by a custom attribute rather than the region source.

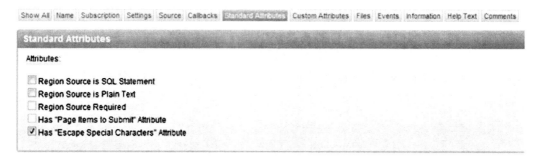

Figure 5-12. Region plug-in standard attributes

Since this plug-in does not require a traditional "Region Source," such as an SQL query or some plain text, you do not need to check those boxes off. If you create a plug-in that requires the user to enter a SQL query as the region source, you can parse the query using the *APEX_PLUGIN_UTIL.GET_DATA* and *APEX_PLUGIN_UTIL.GET_DATA2 function*. For more information, please refer to the APEX API documentation.

Custom Attributes

The following are the custom attributes that the plug-in will use. These attributes are based on the requirements. Specify the attributes for the region using the dialog shown in Figure 5-14, following the list.

- Scope: **Component**
  Attribute:1
  Label: **RSS Type**
  Type: **Select List**
  Required: **Yes**
  Default Value: **Blogger**

- LOVs:
  Display Value: **Blogger**
  Return Value: **Blogger**

  For now, *Blogger* will be the only support RSS feed. If you want to support additional RSS feeds, you can modify this list and the code accordingly.

- Scope: **Component**
  Attribute: **2**
  Label: **RSS URL**
  Type: **Text**
  Required: **Yes**
  Display Width: **50**

- Scope: **Component**
  Attribute: **3**
  Label: **Max Rows**
  Type: **Select List**
  Required: **Yes**
  Default: **5**

- LOVs:
  Display Value: **5**
  Return Value: **5**

  Display Value: **10**
  Return Value: **10**

  Display Value: **15**
  Return Value: **15**

- Scope: **Component**
  Attribute: **4**
  Label: **Modal Width** (controls width of the modal window)
  Type: **Integer**
  Required: **Yes**
  Display Width: **3**
  Maximum Width: **4**
  Default Value: **700**

- Scope: **Component**
  Attribute: **5**
  Label: **Modal Height** (controls height of the modal window)
  Type: **Integer**
  Required: **Yes**
  Display Width: **3**
  Maximum Width: **4**
  Default Value: **400**

You should feel comfortable with and understand the impacts of adding and modifying custom attributes by now. The only difference that you'll experience with region plug-in custom attributes is how they are displayed on the region's edit page.

Instead of being displayed in the usual Settings section, as shown in Figure 5-13, a new tab called Region Attributes contains the custom attributes. Figure 5-14 shows this new tab when modifying a region that is a plug-in region with custom attributes.

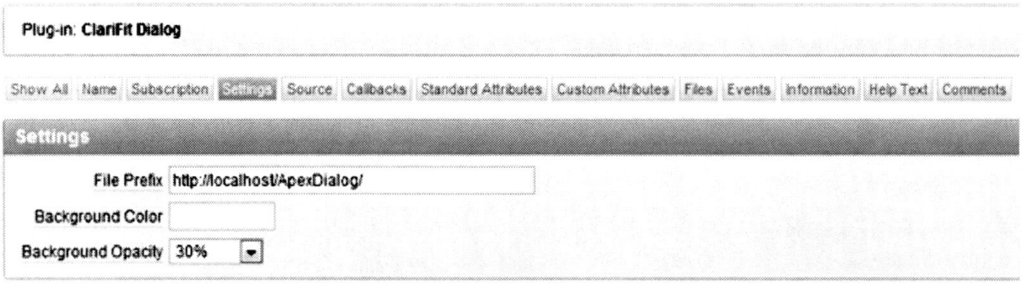

Figure 5-13. Dynamic action plug-in custom attribute settings

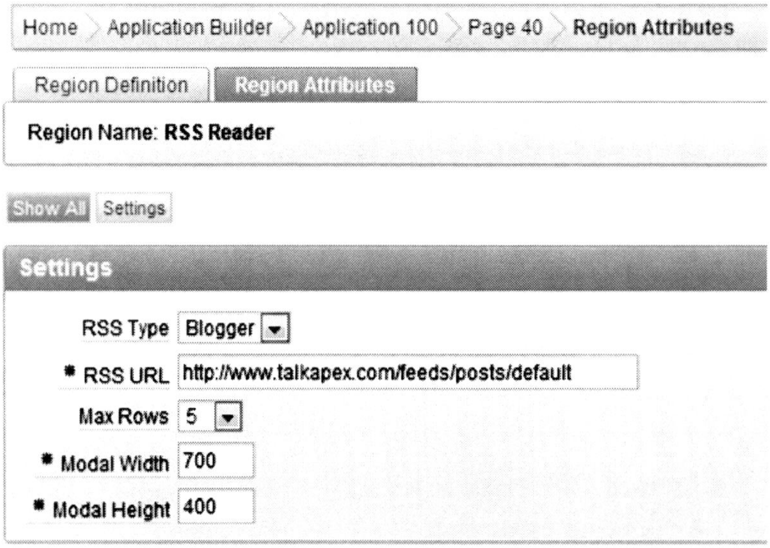

Figure 5-14. Region plug-in custom attribute settings

Creating a Test Page

Before creating the render and AJAX functions, you should set up a test page to help view your changes. The following steps create a test page and a region that uses the new region plug-in:

1. Create a new page with *Page Type* of **Plug-ins**. Click the Next button.

   Just to clarify, there's no such thing as a Page plug-in. In this case, *plug-in* refers to a region plug-in.

2. In the Type page, select **ClariFit RSS Reader** as the *Plug-in.* Click the Next button.

3. On the Page and Region Attributes page, set the following values, then click the Next button to continue.

   Page Number: 40
   Page Name: RSS Reader
   Region Name: RSS Reader

4. On the Tab Options page, click the **Use an existing tab set and create a new tab within the existing tab set** radio button. In the *New Tab Label* field, enter **RSS Reader**. Click the Next button to continue.

5. On the Settings page, leave the default options but set the *RSS URL* to **http://www.talkapex.com/feeds/posts/default**, as shown in Figure 5-15. Click the Next button to continue.

   (Note: You can use any Blogger URL by replacing *www.talkapex.com* with your URL.)

Figure 5-15. RSS Reader settings

6. On the confirmation page, click the Finish button to create the page.

At this point, if you run Page 40, it will display an error message since you have not defined or created a render function, as shown in Figure 5-16. The next section will define and create the region render PL/SQL function.

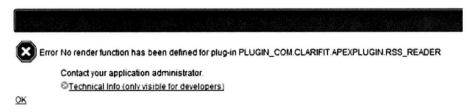

Figure 5-16. No render function error message

Creating the Render Function

Just like the other plug-ins, this plug-in will store its PL/SQL code in the *pkg_apress_plugins* package. To start, get the region plug-in render function template and paste it into *pkg_apress_plugins* spec. Name the render function as f_render_rss_reader. Your *pkg_apress_plugins* package specification should now look like Figure 5-17.

■ **Hint** To get the render function spec template, click render function label and view the help file.

```
1    CREATE OR REPLACE PACKAGE pkg_apress_plugins AS
2
3 ⊞    FUNCTION f_render_from_to_datepicker (...
10
11 ⊞    FUNCTION f_validate_from_to_datepicker (...
16
17 ⊞    FUNCTION f_render_dialog (...
21
22 ⊟    FUNCTION f_render_rss_reader(
23         p_region              IN apex_plugin.t_region,
24         p_plugin              IN apex_plugin.t_plugin,
25         p_is_printer_friendly IN boolean )
26         RETURN apex_plugin.t_region_render_result;
27
28    END pkg_apress_plugins;
29 /
```

Figure 5-17. pkg_apress_plugins.f_render_rss_reader Package Spec

The next thing you'll need to do is register the render function with the plug-in. Edit the plug-in and scroll down to the Callbacks region. Set the *Render Function Name* to **pkg_apress_plugins.f_render_rss_reader**, as shown in Figure 5-18.

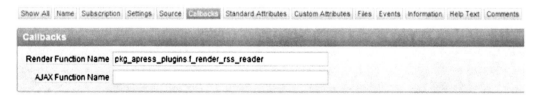

Figure 5-18. Region plug-in callbacks

Modify the package body for pkg_apress_plugins and add the following code at the bottom of code.

```
341 …
342
343 FUNCTION f_render_rss_reader(
344   p_region                IN apex_plugin.t_region,
```

```
345    p_plugin                  IN apex_plugin.t_plugin,
346    p_is_printer_friendly IN boolean )
347    RETURN apex_plugin.t_region_render_result
348 AS
349    -- Region Plugin Attributes
350    v_rss_type apex_application_page_regions.attribute_01%type := p_region.attribute_01; --
blogger (can add more types)
351    v_rss_url apex_application_page_regions.attribute_01%type := p_region.attribute_02;
352    v_max_row_nums pls_integer := to_number(p_region.attribute_03);
353    v_dialog_width apex_application_page_regions.attribute_01%type := p_region.attribute_04;
354    v_dialog_height apex_application_page_regions.attribute_01%type :=
p_region.attribute_05;
355
356    -- Other
357    v_html VARCHAR2(4000); -- Used for temp HTML
358    v_div_id VARCHAR2(255) := 'clarifitRSSReader_' || p_region.id; -- Used for dialog window
placeholder
359    v_rss_xml_namespace VARCHAR2(255);
360
361    -- Return
362    v_return apex_plugin.t_region_render_result;
363
364    -- Procedures
365    PROCEDURE sp_display_rss_title(
366      p_rss_id IN VARCHAR2,
367      p_rss_title IN VARCHAR2,
368      p_rn IN pls_integer, -- Current row number
369      p_row_cnt IN pls_integer -- Total number of rows in the query
370      )
371    AS
372    BEGIN
373      -- Handle first row items
374      IF p_rn = 1 THEN
375        sys.htp.p('<table>');
376      END IF; -- First row
377
378      v_html := ('<tr><td><a
href="javascript:$.clarifitRssReader.showContentModal(''%RSS_ID%'',
clarifitRssReaderVals.R%REGION_ID%);">%TITLE%</a></td></tr>');
379      v_html := REPLACE(v_html, '%TITLE%', p_rss_title);
380      v_html := replace(v_html, '%RSS_ID%', p_rss_id);
381      v_html := REPLACE(v_html, '%REGION_ID%', p_region.id);
382
383      sys.htp.p(v_html);
384
385      -- If Last row close table
386      IF p_rn = p_row_cnt THEN
387        sys.htp.p('</table>');
388      END IF;
389
390    END sp_display_rss_title;
391
```

```
392 BEGIN
393
394    -- Debug information (if app is being run in debug mode)
395    IF apex_application.g_debug THEN
396      apex_plugin_util.debug_region (
397        p_plugin => p_plugin,
398        p_region => p_region,
399        p_is_printer_friendly => p_is_printer_friendly);
400    END IF;
401
402    IF NOT p_is_printer_friendly THEN
403      -- Load JavaSript Files
404      apex_javascript.add_library (p_name => '$console_wrapper', p_directory =>
p_plugin.file_prefix, p_version=> '_1.0.3'); -- Load Console Wrapper for debugging
405      apex_javascript.add_library (p_name => 'clarifitRSSReader', p_directory =>
p_plugin.file_prefix, p_version=> '_1.0.0'); -- Load Console Wrapper for debugging
406
407      -- CSS Properties
408      apex_css.add (
409        p_css => '
410          .clarifitRssReader-label {font-weight: bold}
411          .clarifitRssReader-author {font-style: italic}
412          .clarifitRssReader-link {font-style: italic}
413          ',
414        p_key => 'clarifitRssReader');
415
416      -- Initial JS. Only run if not in printer friendly mode
417      sys.htp.p('<div id="' || v_div_id || '"></div>'); -- Used for dialog placeholder
418
419      -- Set JavaScript global variables that will be used to handle display options
420      sys.htp.p('<script type="text/javascript">(function($){');
421      -- Only run this code once so as not to overwrite the global variable
422      apex_javascript.add_inline_code (
423        p_code => 'var clarifitRssReaderVals = {}',
424        p_key => 'clarifitRssReaderVals');
425
426      -- Extend feature allows you to append variables to JSON object
427      v_html := '
428        $.extend(clarifitRssReaderVals,
429          {"R%REGION_ID%" : {
430            %AJAX_IDENTIFIER%
431            %RSS_TYPE%
432            %IMAGE_PREFIX%
433            %DIALOG_WIDTH%
434            %DIALOG_HEIGHT%
435            %DIV_ID_END_ELEMENT%
436          }});';
437
438      v_html := REPLACE(v_html, '%REGION_ID%', p_region.id);
439      v_html := REPLACE (v_html, '%AJAX_IDENTIFIER%',
apex_javascript.add_attribute('ajaxIdentifier', apex_plugin.get_ajax_identifier));
```

```
440     v_html := REPLACE (v_html, '%RSS_TYPE%', apex_javascript.add_attribute('rssType',
v_rss_type));
441     v_html := REPLACE (v_html, '%IMAGE_PREFIX%',
apex_javascript.add_attribute('imagePrefix', apex_application.g_image_prefix));
442     v_html := REPLACE (v_html, '%DIALOG_WIDTH%',
apex_javascript.add_attribute('dialogWidth', sys.htf.escape_sc(v_dialog_width)));
443     v_html := REPLACE (v_html, '%DIALOG_HEIGHT%',
apex_javascript.add_attribute('dialogHeight', sys.htf.escape_sc(v_dialog_height)));
444     v_html := REPLACE (v_html, '%DIV_ID_END_ELEMENT%',
apex_javascript.add_attribute('divId', v_div_id, FALSE, FALSE));
445
446     apex_javascript.add_inline_code (p_code => v_html);
447
448     sys.htp.p('})(apex.jQuery);</script>');
449   END IF; -- printer friendly
450
451   -- For each type
452   IF v_rss_type = 'blogger' THEN
453     v_rss_xml_namespace := 'http://www.w3.org/2005/Atom';
454
455     FOR x IN (
456       SELECT id, title, rownum rn, count(1) over() row_cnt
457       FROM xmltable(
458           XMLNAMESPACES(DEFAULT 'http://www.w3.org/2005/Atom'),
459           '*' passing httpuritype
(v_rss_url).getxml().EXTRACT('//feed/entry','xmlns="http://www.w3.org/2005/Atom"')
460           COLUMNS id VARCHAR2(4000)   PATH 'id',
461                   title VARCHAR2(48)    PATH 'title',
462                   author   VARCHAR2(1000) path 'author/name'
463                   )
464       WHERE ROWNUM <= v_max_row_nums
465     ) loop
466
467       sp_display_rss_title(
468         p_rss_id => x.ID,
469         p_rss_title => x.title,
470         p_rn => x.rn,
471         p_row_cnt => x.row_cnt);
472     END loop;
473
474   -- Add additional support for RSS feeds here.
475   ELSE
476     -- Unknown RSS type
477     sys.htp.p('Error: unknown RSS type');
478   END IF;
479
480   -- Return
481   RETURN v_return;
482
483 END f_render_rss_reader;
484
485 …
```

The following is a description of the preceding code that is keyed to the line numbers:

349-354: Define the plug-in's attributes and use meaningful variables. All the attributes are strings that need to be explicitly converted to appropriate PL/SQL data types when applicable.

365-390: Reusable internal procedure to display each of the RSS titles in a table format. The titles include links that will trigger some JavaScript code to display the RSS content in a modal window. This will be used to make an AJAX call

395-400: Minimal debug information. Always include some debug information in your plug-in.

402-449: Contains code that is only applicable in normal display mode. The code is there to support the display of the RSS content in a modal window. If the page is run in print mode, then this code is not required.

Line 404 references a JavaScript file that has yet to be created. You will create this file when implementing the AJAX support.

When developing plug-ins with AJAX support, you may tend to initially focus on getting the region to display what you want to display and then add the additional code.

439: This line is very important for AJAX calls. The key component is the reference to the `apex_plugin.get_ajax_identifier` function.

In the AJAX example at the beginning of the chapter, the JavaScript code referenced the PL/SQL code to run by identifying the application process *AJAX_DEMO*. Plug-ins need a similar identifier/reference. The APEX plug-in APIs make things simple so that you don't need to worry about naming this identifier. The `apex_plugin.get_ajax_identifier` function provides a unique name.

451-472: Handle RSS type-specific code to obtain the RSS title and some meta data. Lines 475-476 handle what happens if an unknown RSS type is defined. In this case, it displays a simple error message. How you handle errors is entirely up to you, depending on your business needs. You can use a "soft" error message (as in this case) or a more "harsh" error messages (i.e., raise an application error).

If you run Page 40, it should look like Figure 5-19. Note the values for the RSS feed may vary depending on the URL. If you click on any of the titles, nothing happens as the JavaScript still hasn't been added and the AJAX function has not been defined. This will be covered in the next section.

If you discard the JavaScript specific code, the code for this plug-in is pretty simple and straight forward. The primary responsibility for a region plug-in is to display some content. You don't need to be concerned about items and buttons attached to the region as they are handled as part of the standard APEX region process.

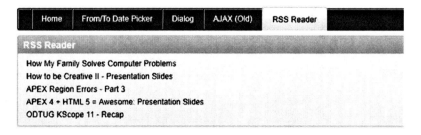

Figure 5-19. RSS Reader rendered

Creating the AJAX Function

This section will add AJAX support to the plug-in. Though this example is for a region plug-in, the concept is the same for other plug-ins that support AJAX calls. Because AJAX involves both server side code (handled by PL/SQL for APEX) and JavaScript code, this section will cover both sets of code.

JavaScript

When working with code that links PL/SQL with JavaScript (and vice versa), it can be difficult to determine whether to start with the client side code (JavaScript) or the server side code (PL/SQL). When dealing with AJAX functions, it is sometimes easier to start with the JavaScript portion. Once the base JavaScript code is working, you start working on the server code. This is usually an iterative process, modifying both JavaScript and the PL/SQL code.

The JavaScript code will use the Console Wrapper JavaScript instrumentation package. To that end, copy **$console_wrapper_1.0.3.js** into in **c:\www\RSSReader**. Then create an empty file named **clarifitRSSReader_1.0.0.js** in **c:\www\RSSReader**. This is the same name that was used in the render function. Open the file and paste in the following code:

■ **Note** This JavaScript code is slightly different from the code used for the previous plug-ins. It does not use the jQuery UI Widget Factory framework.

```
01 (function($){
02
03 $.clarifitRssReader = (function(){
04    var that = {};
05
06    /**
07     * Display the RSS feed's content in a Dialog window
08     */
09    that.showContentModal = function(pRssId, pObj){
10      var scope = '$.clarifitRssReader.showContentModal';
11      $.console.groupCollapsed(scope);
```

```
12      $.console.logParams();
13
14      var $elem = $('#' + pObj.divId);
15
16      //Ensure default options
17      var defaultOptions = {
18        dialogWidth: 700,
19        dialogHeight: 400,
20        modal: true
21        };
22
23      pObj = $.extend(defaultOptions, pObj);
24
25      //Display Loading Message
26      $elem.html('<div style="text-align:center;"><img src="' + pObj.imagePrefix + 'ws/ajax-
loader.gif" style="display: block;margin-left: auto;margin-right: auto"></div>');
27      $elem.dialog({
28        title: 'Loading...',
29        modal: pObj.modal
30      });
31
32      //Prep AJAX call to get HTML content
33      var ajax = new htmldb_Get(null,$v('pFlowId'), 'PLUGIN=' + pObj.ajaxIdentifier,0);
34      ajax.addParam('x01', pObj.rssType);
35      ajax.addParam('x02', pRssId);
36      var ajaxResult = ajax.get();
37
38      var json = $.parseJSON(ajaxResult);
39      $.console.log('json: ', json);
40
41      if (json.errorMsg == ''){
42        //No Error message, display content
43        //Modify content to include some additional information about the rss post
44        json.content = '<span class="clarifitRssReader-label">By</span>:<span
class="clarifitRssReader-author">' + json.author + '</span><br>' + '<span
class="clarifitRssReader-label">Link</span>: ' + '<a href="' + json.link + '" target="blank"
class="clarifitRssReader-link">' + json.link + '</a><br><br>' + json.content;
45
46        //Display in Modal window
47        $elem.dialog('close'); //close Loading messsage
48        $elem.html(json.content);
49        $elem.dialog({
50          title: json.title,
51          width:  pObj.dialogWidth,
52          height: pObj.dialogHeight,
53          modal: pObj.modal
54        });
55        $.console.groupEnd(scope);
56      }
57      else {
58        //Error occurred
59        $elem.dialog('close'); //close Loading messsage
```

```
60        $elem.html('An error occurred loading RSS feed');
61        $elem.dialog({
62          title: 'Error',
63          width:  pObj.dialogWidth,
64          height: pObj.dialogHeight,
65          modal: pObj.modal
66        });
67      }//error message
68
69    };//showContentModal
70
71    return that;
72 })();//$clarifitRssReader
73
74 })(apex.jQuery);
```

The following is a description of the preceding code that is keyed to the line numbers:

> **1 & 74**: Like other JavaScript code, this block of JavaScript explicitly defines the jQuery namespace but leverages the version of jQuery that is part of APEX.
>
> **26-30**: Displays a "Loading..." message when the user clicks on a RSS title and is waiting for the server to respond.
>
> **32-36**: This is what actually makes the AJAX call. This code is very similar to the example code covered in the Background > AJAX section at the beginning of this chapter. The major difference is that on line 33, instead of referencing an application process by *APPLICATION_PROCESS*, it references the plug-in process by *PLUGIN*. The name of the plug-in AJAX identifier is defined in the region's render function with a call to `apex_plugin.get_ajax_identifier` (refer back to the render function).
>
> **38**: The response from the server comes back as a string. Since it is really a JSON object, you need to explicitly convert it to a JavaScript JSON object. If you are expecting a non-string value, you will always need to explicitly convert it.
>
> **41-67**: Displays the RSS content (received from the AJAX call) in a modal window or the error message accordingly.

Refresh Page 40 and click on one of the RSS links. Look in the console window and you should see the POST request, as shown in Figure 5-20. You can see the values that are passed to APEX (*x01* and *x02*) that will be used in your PL/SQL AJAX render function.

If you click on the Response tab, you'll see that a bunch of HTML was returned. Scanning through the HTML, you'll notice that the content is essentially a standard error page in APEX. The error message is "*No AJAX function has been defined for plug-in PLUGIN_COM.CLARIFIT.APEXPLUGIN.RSS_READER,*" as shown in Figure 5-21. This makes sense as you still have not defined an AJAX function for the plug-in. If you ever get a similar response while developing AJAX support for a plug-in, it helps to scan through the returned HTML to see what is going wrong.

Figure 5-20. AJAX POST request

Figure 5-21. AJAX error message

Writing the AJAX Callback Function

Now that the JavaScript code is complete and "talking" to APEX, it's time to define the server side code. The first thing is to do is create the function specification and register it with the plug-in:

1. Edit the plug-in and scroll down to the Callbacks region. Click on the AJAX Function Name label to view the help text. Similar to render functions, AJAX function header templates are provided in the help text. Copy the function header for region type plug-ins as shown in Figure 5-22.

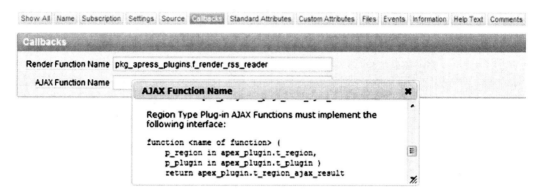

Figure 5-22. AJAX function help

2. Paste the function template into the package spec for pkg_apress_plugins. Name the function f_ajax_rss_reader and compile the package spec.

3. To register the function with the plug-in, edit the plug-in and scroll down to the Callbacks section. Enter **pkg_apress_plugins.f_ajax_rss_reader** in the *AJAX Function Name* field. Click the Apply Changes button to save your change.

The final step is to enter the code for the package body. Edit the package body for pkg_apress_plugins and copy the following code at the bottom of the package:

```
484 …
485
486 FUNCTION f_ajax_rss_reader (
487   p_region IN apex_plugin.t_region,
488   p_plugin IN apex_plugin.t_plugin )
489   RETURN apex_plugin.t_region_ajax_result
490 AS
491   -- APEX Application Variables (x01..x10)
492   v_rss_type VARCHAR2(255) := LOWER(apex_application.g_x01);
493   v_rss_id VARCHAR2(255) := apex_application.g_x02;
494
495   -- Region Plugin Attributes
496   v_rss_url apex_application_page_regions.attribute_01%TYPE := p_region.attribute_02;
497
498   -- Other Variables
499   v_author VARCHAR2(255);
500   v_title VARCHAR2(255);
501   v_link VARCHAR2(1000);
```

```
502    v_content CLOB;
503    v_cnt pls_integer;
504
505    -- Return
506    v_return apex_plugin.t_region_ajax_result;
507
508    -- Functions
509
510    -- Prints HTML JSON object for page to process
511    PROCEDURE sp_print_json(
512      p_author IN VARCHAR2,
513      p_title IN VARCHAR,
514      p_content IN CLOB,
515      p_link IN VARCHAR2,
516      p_error_msg IN VARCHAR2 DEFAULT NULL)
517
518    AS
519      v_html CLOB;
520      v_content clob;
521    BEGIN
522      v_content := p_content;
523
524      -- Escape HTML if required
525      IF p_region.escape_output THEN
526        v_content := sys.htf.escape_sc(v_content);
527      END IF;
528
529      v_html := '{
530        %AUTHOR%
531        %TITLE%
532        %CONTENT%
533        %LINK%
534        %ERROR_MSG_END_ELEMENT%
535      }';
536
537      v_html := REPLACE(v_html, '%AUTHOR%', apex_javascript.add_attribute('author',
sys.htf.escape_sc(p_author), FALSE));
538      v_html := REPLACE(v_html, '%TITLE%', apex_javascript.add_attribute('title',
sys.htf.escape_sc(p_title), FALSE));
539      v_html := REPLACE(v_html, '%CONTENT%', apex_javascript.add_attribute('content',
v_content, FALSE));
540      v_html := REPLACE(v_html, '%LINK%', apex_javascript.add_attribute('link',
sys.htf.escape_sc(p_link), FALSE));
541      v_html := REPLACE(v_html, '%ERROR_MSG_END_ELEMENT%',
apex_javascript.add_attribute('errorMsg', sys.htf.escape_sc(p_error_msg), FALSE, FALSE));
542
543      sys.htp.p(v_html);
544    END sp_print_json;
545
546    -- Wrapper for error message
547    PROCEDURE sp_print_error_msg(
548      p_error_msg IN VARCHAR2)
```

```
549    AS
550    BEGIN
551      sp_print_json(
552        p_author => NULL,
553        p_title => NULL,
554        p_content => NULL,
555        p_link => null,
556        p_error_msg => p_error_msg);
557    END sp_print_error_msg;
558
559  BEGIN
560
561    IF v_rss_type = 'blogger' THEN
562      -- Get blog details
563      DECLARE
564        http_request_failed EXCEPTION;
565        PRAGMA EXCEPTION_INIT(http_request_failed, -29273);
566      BEGIN
567        SELECT author, title, CONTENT, LINK
568        INTO v_author, v_title, v_content, v_link
569        FROM xmltable(
570            XMLNAMESPACES(DEFAULT 'http://www.w3.org/2005/Atom'),
571            '*' passing httpuritype
(v_rss_url).getxml().EXTRACT('//feed/entry','xmlns="http://www.w3.org/2005/Atom"')
572            COLUMNS ID VARCHAR2(4000) path 'id',
573                    title VARCHAR2(48) path 'title',
574                    link VARCHAR2(1000) path 'link[@rel="alternate"]/@href',
575                    author VARCHAR2(1000) path 'author/name',
576                    content CLOB PATH 'content')
577        WHERE ID = v_rss_id;
578
579        sp_print_json(
580          p_author => v_author,
581          p_title => v_title,
582          p_content => v_content,
583          p_link => v_link);
584
585      EXCEPTION
586        WHEN NO_DATA_FOUND THEN
587          sp_print_error_msg(p_error_msg => 'Invalid RSS ID');
588        WHEN TOO_MANY_ROWS THEN
589          sp_print_error_msg(p_error_msg => 'RSS ID returned multiple matches');
590        WHEN http_request_failed THEN
591          sp_print_error_msg(p_error_msg => 'HTTP Connection Error');
592        WHEN OTHERS THEN
593          sp_print_error_msg(p_error_msg => 'Unknown Error');
594      END; -- Select
595
596    -- Add more RSS type support here
597    ELSE
598      -- Return error message
599      sp_print_error_msg(p_error_msg => 'Unknown RSS Type');
```

```
600   END IF; -- v_rss_type
601
602   RETURN v_return;
603
604 EXCEPTION
605   WHEN OTHERS THEN
606     sp_print_error_msg(p_error_msg => 'Unknown Error');
607 END f_ajax_rss_reader;
608 …
```

The following is a description of the preceding code that is keyed to the line numbers:

491-493: Meaningful variable names for values passed in as part of POST request. Remember these variables have nothing to do with plug-in specific attributes.

495-496: Plug-in specific variables.

505: The return object contains a dummy attribute. The only thing to really "return" is what is printed back using `htp.p` calls.

510-544: Reusable function to print out a JSON object with all the applicable data that the JavaScript function will use to display the RSS content in a modal window. This function is essentially what sends data back to the client's browser.

524-527: Escapes special characters from the RSS content based on the region's escape option. This will play a factor in how the content is displayed to the user. You will see exactly how this impacts the application when testing the plug-in.

546-557: Wrapper function to handle errors. In this example, errors will be handled by the JavaScript function. How you handle AJAX errors is your decision; however, you should make sure that that the application is still useable.

559-607: Code to obtain the contents of an RSS feed.

Testing the Plug-in

The final thing to do is test the final product. Refresh Page 40. It should look like it did in Figure 5-19. If you click on one of the RSS titles, a modal window will appear and display the content from the RSS feed, as shown in Figure 5-23.

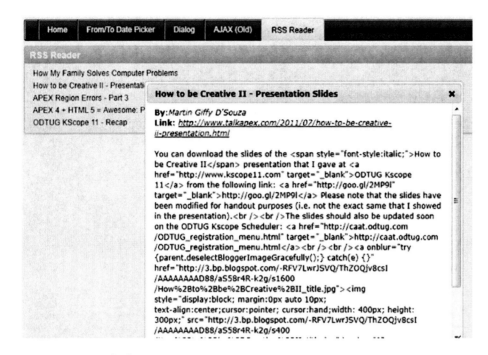

Figure 5-23. RSS feed content

The first thing that stands out in Figure 5-23 is that the content shows all the HTML tags rather than being in a human readable format. This is because of the region's *Escape Special Characters* option, which is currently set to its default value: *Yes.*

To change this option (and you should only do so if the RSS feed is from a trusted source), edit the region and scroll down to the Security section. Set the *Escape Special Characters* to **No**, as shown in Figure 5-24. Run Page 40 and click on the same link as before. The content is a lot more human readable now, as shown in Figure 5-25.

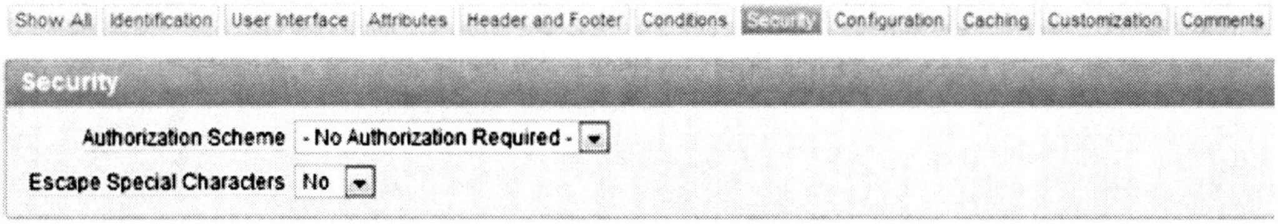

Figure 5-24. Region security settings

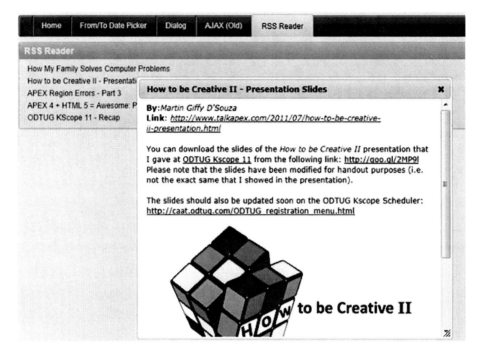

Figure 5-25. RSS feed content (unescaped)

Summary

This chapter provided some background information to help you understand what is required for a region plug-in and how AJAX works in APEX. You also built a region plug-in that contained an AJAX function.

■ **Note** This plug-in did not embed the code or the external files into the plug-in. If you want to do so, please refer to the Item plug-in chapter.

CHAPTER 6

Process Plug-ins

The last type of plug-in that will be covered in this book is the Process type plug-in. This chapter will also cover process plug-ins, when to use/develop them, and provide an example of them.

A process plug-in is a plug-in that executes a block of PL/SQL using the APEX plug-in architecture. Like all APEX processes, they can be run anywhere on a page where a page process can run. This includes both during page load and during page processing (when the page is submitted). Because of this, process plug-ins may be used for both display purposes and processing data (though it is not common to use it for display content).

PL/SQL Region vs. Process Plug-in

One of the most common questions people tend to have when first looking at process plug-ins is *Why?* For example, why would you need a process plug-in when you can just write a stored procedure and reference it in a page process? This is an excellent and justified question.

They're a few reasons why you'd need to create a process plug-in over using a PL/SQL procedure:

> **Reusability:** If you plan to make your plug-in public or share across domains within an organization that do not have access to your current code base (i.e. schema), you'll need a simple and easy way to store the code. By using a plug-in, you can bundle all the code together.

> **Hide Complexity:** Similar to the previous reason, some process plug-ins can get complex. For example, if dealing with some web services, it may easier to store it all in a plug-in so that other developers don't need to worry about any complex code that may be required.

In the example that follows, we'll create a plug-in that masks some complexity/business logic and can be reused.

Business Problem

Always take time to review the business problem that a plugin is trying to resolve. Make that your common practice.

In this case, developers would like a process to quickly send text messages to a specific cellphone. Here is the list of requirements:

- Send a text message to specified cell phone.

- Specify parameters that include carrier info, phone number, and message.

- Support cell phones using Telus, Rogers, and AT&T providers.

■ **Note** Normally you would use a web service that would handle which carrier a number belongs to and send the text message directly to that carrier's messaging service. To simplify things, the example plug-in requires that the APEX developer pass the name of the cell phone carrier/provider for the cell phone number.

Building the Process Plug-in

This section will leverage the requirements listed in the previous section to build a process type plug-in. This plug-in will send text messages to cell phones by emailing specific email addresses based on the cell phone provider.

Resolving Technical Requirements

This plug-in will leverage the APEX_MAIL package to send emails (which will be forwarded to the cell phone by the cell phone provider). You will need to ensure that your APEX instance is properly configured to send emails. The following steps describe how to configure APEX with your SMTP (email) server.

■ **Note** These steps require admin access to the APEX administration (internal) workspace. You may need to ask your DBA to provide you with admin access. You may also need to ask your IT administrator for the correct SMTP server settings.

---

1. As shown in Figure 6-1, log into the *INTERNAL* workspace used to manage the APEX instance on a database.

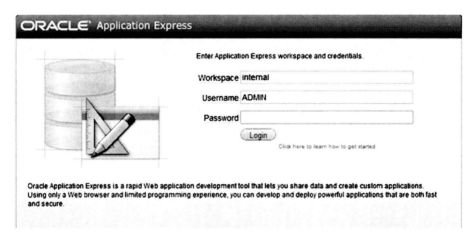

Figure 6-1. Internal Workspace Login

2. As shown in Figure 6-2, click on the *Manage Instance* button.

Figure 6-2. APEX Internal Workspace

3. In the Instance Settings region, click on the *Instance Settings* link as shown in Figure 6-3.

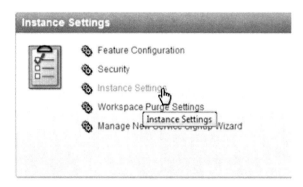

Figure 6-3. Manage Instance

4. In the Instance Settings page, scroll down to the Email region as shown in Figure 6-4. Enter the appropriate SMTP server information. The figure omits an example SMTP server and related details because all that information is specific to your own environment. Once you are finished, click Apply Changes.

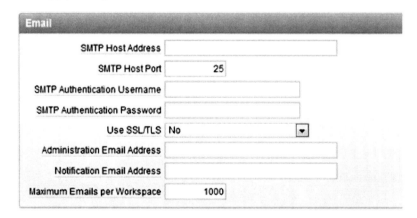

Figure 6-4. Email SMTP Configuration

It's important to note that APEX does not send emails immediately. Instead it will queue up emails and periodically send them based on a scheduled job. You can manually "push" emails off the queue by using the *APEX_MAIL.PUSH_QUEUE* procedure.

Setting up Initial Configuration

Create a new process plug-in with the following attributes:

Name: **ClariFitText Message**

Internal Name: **COM.CLARIFIT.APEXPLUGIN.TEXT_MSG**

*Type:***Process**

*Execution Function Name:***pkg_apress_plugins.f_execute_txt_msg**

The Execution Function Name references a procedure that has yet to be created. The procedure will be created in the Execution Function section below.

You'll notice that process plug-ins don't have many default configurable settings. This is because page processes run PL/SQL code and don't require a lot of attributes.

Adding Custom Attributes

The following steps list the custom attributes that the plug-in will use. These attributes are based on the requirements. Please create the following attributes for the plug-in:

- Scope: **Application**
  Attribute:**1**
  Label:**Force Push Mail Queue**
  Type: **Yes/No**
  Required: **Yes**
  Default Value: **Y**

- Scope:**Component**
  Attribute:**1**
  Label:**Phone Number**
  Type:**Text**
  Required:**Yes**
  Display Width:**30**
  Maximum Width:**60**

  North American phone numbers only require 10 digits, however it makes sense to leave the phone number width to more than 10 characters since an APEX developer will probably reference a page item and use a substitution string that may easily exceed 10 characters. The same is true for the attributes listed below. This will be highlighted on the test page.

- Scope: **Component**
  Attribute:**2**
  Label:**Carrier Code**
  Type: **Text**
  Required:**Yes**
  Display Width:**30**
  Maximum Width:**60**

- Scope: **Component**
  Attribute:**3**
  Label:**Text Message**
  Type: **Textarea**
  Required:**Yes**

Execution Function

Just like the other plug-ins, the first thing to do is retrieve the function header information from the help text on the plug-in page. Using the header template, add the following lines to the specification of pkg_apress_plugins and recompile it.

```
FUNCTION f_execute_txt_msg (
  p_process IN apex_plugin.t_process,
  p_plugin  IN apex_plugin.t_plugin )
  RETURN apex_plugin.t_process_exec_result;
```

Modify the package body for pkg_apress_plugins and add the following code at the bottom of the body. A detailed description follows the code.

```
610 …
611 FUNCTION f_execute_txt_msg (
612   p_process IN apex_plugin.t_process,
613   p_plugin  IN apex_plugin.t_plugin )
614   RETURN apex_plugin.t_process_exec_result
615 AS
616
617   -- Types
618   TYPE typ_carrier_info IS record (
619     email_addr VARCHAR2(255),
620     num_digits NUMBER(2,0) --If null then any list of numbers will work
621   );
622
623   TYPE tt_carrier_info IS TABLE OF typ_carrier_info  INDEX BY varchar2(10); -- index by
carrier code
624
625
626   -- Application Plugin Attributes
627   v_force_push_queue_flag apex_application_page_items.attribute_01%TYPE :=
upper(p_plugin.attribute_01); -- force pushing the APEX mail queue
628
629   -- Item Plugin Attributes
630   v_phone_number apex_application_page_items.attribute_01%TYPE := p_process.attribute_01;
631   v_carrier_code apex_application_page_items.attribute_01%TYPE :=
upper(p_process.attribute_02); -- Cell phone carrier code
632   v_txt_msg apex_application_page_items.attribute_01%TYPE := p_process.attribute_03; --
Text message to send
633
634   -- Other variables
635   v_return apex_plugin.t_process_exec_result;
636   v_all_carrier_info tt_carrier_info;
637
638   v_carrier_info typ_carrier_info; -- Current carrier info
639
640   -- Functions
641   FUNCTION f_ret_carrier_info_rec(
642     p_email_addr VARCHAR2,
643     p_num_digits NUMBER)
644     RETURN typ_carrier_info
```

148

```
645   AS
646     v_carrier_info typ_carrier_info;
647   BEGIN
648     v_carrier_info.email_addr := p_email_addr;
649     v_carrier_info.num_digits := p_num_digits;
650     RETURN v_carrier_info;
651   END;
652
653 BEGIN
654   -- Debug
655   IF apex_application.g_debug THEN
656     apex_plugin_util.debug_process (
657       p_plugin => p_plugin,
658       p_process => p_process);
659   END IF;
660
661   -- Remove non numeric values from phone number
662   -- This allows phone numbers to be in any format
663   v_phone_number := regexp_replace(v_phone_number, '[^[:digit:]]', '');
664
665   -- Load Carrier info
666   -- Email addresses obtained from: http://www.emailtextmessages.com/
667   v_all_carrier_info('TELUS') := f_ret_carrier_info_rec(p_email_addr =>
'@NUM@@msg.telus.com', p_num_digits => 10);
668   v_all_carrier_info('ROGERS') := f_ret_carrier_info_rec(p_email_addr =>
'@NUM@@pcs.rogers.com', p_num_digits => 10);
669   v_all_carrier_info('ATT') := f_ret_carrier_info_rec(p_email_addr => '@NUM@@txt.att.net',
p_num_digits => 10);
670   -- Can add more carrier code information here
671
672   -- Set current carrier
673   BEGIN
674     v_carrier_info := v_all_carrier_info(v_carrier_code);
675     v_carrier_info.email_addr := REPLACE(v_carrier_info.email_addr, '@NUM@',
v_phone_number); -- Replace mnemonic
676   EXCEPTION
677     WHEN NO_DATA_FOUND THEN
678       raise_application_error(-20001, 'Invalid carrier code');
679   END;
680
681   -- VALIDATIONS
682   IF v_phone_number IS NULL THEN
683     raise_application_error(-20001, 'Missing phone number');
684   elsif v_carrier_info.num_digits IS NOT NULL AND v_carrier_info.num_digits !=
LENGTH(v_phone_number) THEN
685     raise_application_error(-20001, 'Number of digits is incorrect. Have: ' ||
v_phone_number || '. Expected: ' || v_carrier_info.num_digits);
686   END IF;
687
688   -- Send meail to text message
689   apex_mail.send(
690     p_to => v_carrier_info.email_addr,
```

```
691      p_from => NULL,
692      p_body => v_txt_msg);
693
694    -- Push mail queue only if necessary
695    IF v_force_push_queue_flag = 'Y' THEN
696      -- Send text message right away
697      apex_mail.push_queue();
698    END IF;
699
700    -- Return
701    v_return.success_message := p_process.success_message;
702    RETURN v_return;
703
704 END f_execute_txt_msg;
705...
```

The following is a description of the preceding code that is keyed to line numbers:

622-632: Plug-in attributes. Just like the other examples from previous chapters, it helps to convert them into meaningful names rather than reference them throughout your code using the attribute numbers.

640-651: Since some plug-ins may not have any dependencies on other code in the database, you can store functions and procedures directly inside the plug-in function. You can also store the additional function and procedures in the plug-in source region.

654-659: All plug-ins should include the appropriate debug code. There's really no reason why they shouldn't include debug statements.

663: This regular expression converts the phone number into digits. When applicable, this is a good technique since it allows end users to enter in phone numbers in any format they like. For example (123) 456-7890 and 123-456-7890 will both be converted to 1234567890. This technique also helps the APEX developer since they don't need to explicitly convert the phone number to a special format to work with the plug-in. You can use this technique for other types of inputs as well.

672-686: Determines the email address to use for the text message. The important thing to note is how the errors are handled. Since it doesn't make sense to continue with the process if the text messages aren't sent, an application level error is raised. The error will be handled by the standard APEX error handling process.

701: You can define your own success message or use the one that the user provided in the Process Success Message text area as shown in Figure 6-5.

Figure 6-5. Process Messages

You'll notice that they're a lot of similarities with this code compared to the other three plug-ins from the previous chapters. It declares variables (assigning logical names to plug-in attributes), calls the APEX plug-in debug statement (when running in debug mode), processes the information, and then does something (in this case, emails the phone carrier the text message).

Compared to the other plug-ins, the major difference with this plug-in is that it does not actually display anything. Since it is a process plug-in, it can be run when the page is being processed and it may not make sense to actually display anything. The only feedback to the end user is the *success message* (defined on line 701), which will be displayed to the end user if one is specified.

Testing it Out

Now that you've built the process plug-in, the last thing to do is ensure it works. The following steps will walk you through building an example page that utilizes this plug-in:

1. Using the page creation wizard, create a new page with the following attribute:

   *Type:***Blank Page**
   *Page Number:***60**
   *Name:***Text Message**
   *HTML Region 1:***Text Message**
   New Tab: **Text Message**

2. Edit Page 60. In the *Text Message* region, create the following page items:

   a. *Type:***Select List**
   Item Name: **P60_CARRIER_CODE**
   *Value Required:***Yes**
   LOV-Display Null Value:- **Select Carrier -**
   *LOV-Query:***STATIC2:Telus;TELUS,Rogers;ROGERS,ATT;AT&T**

    b.   *Type:* Text **Field**
        *Item Name:***P60_PHONE_NUMBER**
        Value Required: **Yes**

    c.   *Type:* Text **Area**
        *Item Name:***P60_TEXT_MSG**
        Value Required: **Yes**
        *Character Counter:***Yes**

3.   In the *Text Message* region, create a region button with the following attributes:

*Button Name:***SEND_TEXT_MESSAGE**
*Label:***Send Text Message**
Position: **Bottom of Region**
*Alignment:***Left**
Action: Submit **Page**
*Execute Validations:***Yes**

4.   Create a Page Process to send the text message (and use the plug-in). These steps include screen shots, as they have not been covered in earlier sections.

    a.   In the Page Processing region, right click on the Processing tree element and select **Create Process** as shown in Figure 6-1.

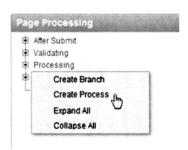

Figure 6-6. Create Page Process

    b.   For the *Process Type,* select **Plug-ins**.

    c.   Select **ClariFit Send Text Message.**

d. On the Process Attributes page, enter Send Text Message in the Name field as shown in Figure 6-7. Click the Next button to continue.

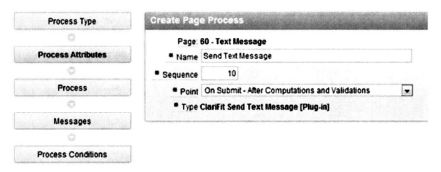

Figure 6-7. Create Page Process: Process Attributes

e. The Process displays the custom attributes for the plug-in. In some cases, you may hard code in the values. In this example, you'll use user-defined values that reference the appropriate page items using substitution strings. Enter the values as shown in Figure 6-8.

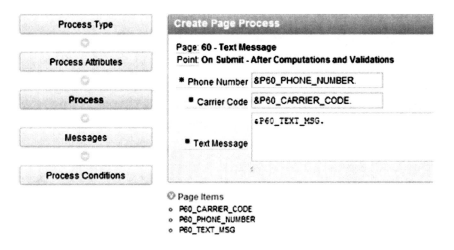

Figure 6-8. Create Page Process: Process

    f.   On the Messages page, enter in the following values:

    *Success Message:***Text message sent.**
    *Error Message:***Error sending text message.**

    These values are not required but are recommended since it will notify the end user.

    g.   On the Process Conditions page, select **SEND_TEXT_MESSAGE** for the *When Button Pressed* option and click the Create Process button to complete the wizard.

■ **Note** In step 4.e, the width of the phone number attribute is not restricted to 10 characters (for North American numbers). Since substitution strings may be used and the substitution string may exceed 10 characters, it would not make sense to restrict the input length. You should keep this in mind when setting restrictions on attributes for process plug-ins.

To test out the process, run Page 60. Enter the appropriate information and click the Send Text Message button. The page will be submitted and you should see a success message as shown in Figure 6-9.

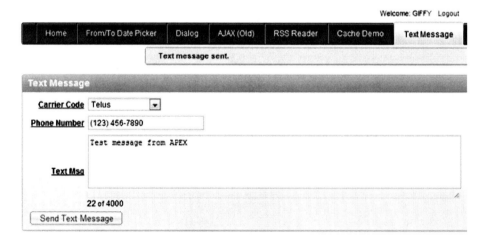

Figure 6-9. Text Message Example

■ **Note** The phone number can be entered using any type of format. That's because the plug-in extracts only the numbers and uses that for the email address. When developing plug-ins, you may want to consider making some attributes' formats irrelevant where applicable.

Summary

This chapter covered how to build a process plug-in and when you would do so instead of using a PL/SQL process referencing a procedure.

This plug-in did not embed the code into the plug-in because it was already covered. For process type plug-ins, you would normally embed the PL/SQL code since the plug-in would most likely be shared.

■ ■ ■

CHAPTER 7

Best Practices & Community

As with all programming languages and frameworks, there are some best practices to help developers create solid and robust plug-ins. These best practices are just recommendations and can vary by organization depending on your individual requirements. You may find that some of the best practices described in this chapter are not worded exactly as they are in your organization. That's perfectly fine, as they are meant to be a guideline. Adopt them as necessary to suit your team's needs.

APEX has a vibrant and vocal development community. When plug-ins were first introduced, various plug in–specific web sites were created to help share plug-ins and demonstrate different techniques. Reach out to this community when you need support. Give back when you are able to provide support for others.

■ **Note** Special thanks to Patrick Wolf and Dan McGhan for providing some of their thoughts for this chapter.

When to Create a Plug-in

So, when exactly do you create a plug-in? This is a very common question that developers ask about plug-ins. The answer is, as Oracle guru Tom Kyte would say, "It depends." There's no set answer, but the following are some things to consider when responding to the question:

> *Time*: i.e., do you have the time to write this plug-in? If you're in a time crunch, you may not be able to spend the time writing a full-blown plug-in. Alternatively, if you have time restrictions, you may consider writing a plug-in with the minimal set of features to get you going. When you have more time, then you can go back and add additional features as required.

> *Cost of not writing plug-in*: What would be the cost of not writing a plug-in? Sometimes, writing a plug-in may seem like extra work and unnecessary when you're pressed for time. If you're doing a bunch of hacks just to avoid writing a plug-in, then it will probably cost you more in the long run. This is similar to the idiom "one step forward, two steps back."

Reusability. As with code modularization, if you plan to reuse certain functionality and it makes sense to do so, write a plug-in. If you're unsure in a particular situation, hold off and wait to see if you reuse the same code somewhere else. If so, then you should probably write a plug-in. The main thing to remember is not to start creating your own custom framework for a workaround when one already exists.

Moving parts. If without a plug-in your code has to make a lot of assumptions and has a lot of *moving parts*, you may want to write a plug-in. Encapsulating all of the code in a single location will allow you to better control how things.

It is also important not to get carried away by developing plug-ins for things that are already supported. For instance, you should not write a dynamic action plug-in for a browser alert message.

Be Aware About Security

One side effect of creating your own plug-ins is that you may introduce various security exploits in your application without knowing it. The following subsections discuss some common security mistakes and how to avoid them when creating a plug-in.

Cross-Site Scripting Attacks

Cross-site scripting, commonly referred to as XSS, is when a user puts malicious JavaScript code on your web site to silently steal information. A good opportunity for this is an application which allows users to enter comments at the bottom of the page. When other users view the page, they'll see the comments posted by all users. If the comment values are not escaped, a malicious user can put code into a comment which can send the malicious user private information about any user currently logged in.

To prevent users from entering code into text fields and having that code executed, you can escape user input when it's being displayed. To do this you can use the `APEX_PLUGIN_UTIL.ESCAPE` function. Instead of always forcing escaped values, you should use the plug-in *escape* variable. For example, in item type plug-ins, APEX developers can choose to escape the values as shown in Figure 7-. The value of the `Escape special characters` checkbox in the figure is reflected in the corresponding `p_item.escape_output` variable accessible from within the plug-in functions.

■ **Note** For more information about cross-site scripting in general, please read
`http://en.wikipedia.org/wiki/Cross-site_scripting`.

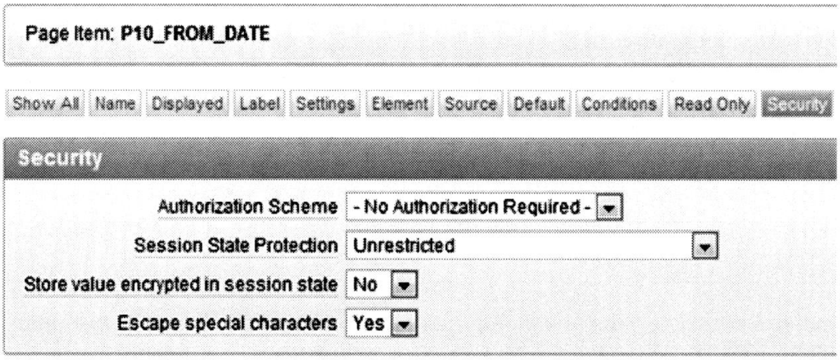

Page Item: P10_FROM_DATE										

| Show All | Name | Displayed | Label | Settings | Element | Source | Default | Conditions | Read Only | Security |

Security

Authorization Scheme	- No Authorization Required - ▾
Session State Protection	Unrestricted ▾
Store value encrypted in session state	No ▾
Escape special characters	Yes ▾

Figure 7-1. Escape special characters

SQL Injection Attacks

SQL injection happens when a user enters a SQL statement, or a fragment of a statement, in an input value with the intent of trying to expose security holes in an application. A simple example can be built around an "execute immediate" block of PL/SQL used to invalidate a user input item. Suppose you had a page item, P1_NAME, that used a plug-in item to call an execute immediate block using the item value as part of the validation. The execute immediate invocation would look like the following:

```
execute immediate 'BEGIN some_validation_procedure (p_name => ''' || p_value || '''); END;';
```

If the p_value is "Martin", the execute immediate block will run the following code:

```
BEGIN some_validation_procedure (p_name => 'Martin'); END;
```

At first glance, the preceding code and the example look good, but what if the user enters some malicious code in the item value? For example, what if the user enters '); TRUNCATE TABLE users; --? The execute immediate block will then run the following code:

```
BEGIN some_validation_procedure (p_name => ''); TRUNCATE TABLE users; --'); END;
```

You'll notice that this code will call some_validation_procedure, and then truncate a table. Besides dropping a table, a malicious user can obtain all your data using the right techniques. SQL injection is clearly something you want to guard against.

APEX has some functions that, when used properly, can prevent SQL injection.

- APEX_PLUGIN_UTIL.EXECUTE_PLSQL_CODE

- APEX_PLUGIN_UTIL.GET_DATA(2)

- APEX_PLUGIN_UTIL.GET_DISPLAY_DATA(2)

- APEX_PLUGIN_UTIL.GET_PLSQL_EXPRESSION_RESULT

- APEX_PLUGIN_UTIL.GET_PLSQL_FUNCTION_RESULT

It's recommended that you use these functions when needed, both for security reasons and to make your coding easier, as these functions and procedures will also enable all bind variables. For more information, read the APEX_PLUGIN_UTIL API documentation.

Using the `APEX_PLUGIN_UTIL.EXECUTE_PLSQL_CODE` procedure to rewrite the previous example, the execute immediate call would look like the following:

```
apex_plugin_util.execute_plsql_code(p_plsql_code => 'BEGIN some_validation_procedure (p_name
=> :' || v_page_item_name || '); END;';
```

In this case, a bind variable is used to pass in the p_name parameter.
The `APEX_PLUGIN_UTIL.EXECUTE_PLSQL_CODE` procedure will automatically bind the value for you.

Protect Sensitive Information

It's important not to put sensitive information in code that is accessible to end users. A classic example of this is having an AJAX function that updates a table with a value as follows:

```
//AJAX JavaScript Function
var ajax = new htmldb_Get(null,$v('pFlowId'), 'PLUGIN=' + pObj.ajaxIdentifier,0);
ajax.addParam('x01', 'my_table'); // Table to update
ajax.addParam('x02', 'my_column'); // Some column
ajax.addParam('x03', 'some_value'); // Some column
ajax.addParam('x04', 'my_pk_column = 123'); // Column to update
var ajaxResult = ajax.get();

-- Corresponding PL/SQL Procedure
l_sql :=
   ' UPDATE ' || apex_application.g_x01 ||
   ' SET ' || apex_application.g_x02 || ' = ''' || apex_application.g_x03 || '''' ||
   ' WHERE ' || apex_application.g_x03;

execute immediate l_sql;
```

If a malicious user looks at the preceding JavaScript code, which is currently accessible, the user can obtain two pieces of information. The first is at least one table in your schema. Using this information, the user can guess some other tables in your schema. More importantly, he/she can update any value by simply modifying the JavaScript code.

Instead of using the previously shown technique, you should re-evaluate what you're trying to accomplish and move as much business logic back into the plug-in as possible. All you should allow end users to specify is the value. The meta data—i.e., the table, column, and row to update—should remain in the plug-in.

Instrument Your Code

Code instrumentation has been mentioned throughout this book. If mentioning it again seems repetitive, it is. Regardless of what language you are programming in, instrumenting your code will always pay off in the end. This is especially true when you encounter issues in production level plug-ins.

If you bundle your plug-ins (i.e., include all the code directly in the plug-in), then having the ability to receive debug information from other developers is critical. If you do not develop your plug-ins with this in mind, it can be very difficult to debug a remote issue.

The examples in this book use code instrumentation both in the JavaScript and the PL/SQL blocks. Only a minimal number of debug statements were added to help with the readability of the code. You are encouraged to add additional debug statements using the APEX_DEBUG_MESSAGE package or your own, internal, debugging, and logging package.

For more information on how to instrument your code and view the results of adding the debug statements, read the upcoming Chapter 8 on debugging and tools.

Comment Your Code

Another standard development best practice is to comment your code. This is a principle that should go without saying. Someone else will eventually work on, or look at, your code. This is especially true with plug-ins, as they are meant to be reusable.

Since some plug-ins are tightly integrated with JavaScript, it helps to comment on how certain features may be interpreted/used by JavaScript. For example, in a render function, if you're adding specific code that will be used by a JavaScript function, then state *why* you are adding that code. Your comments will help programmers who follow you in working on that code.

On the JavaScript side, state what sort of data you expect from the plug-in, both during initialization and during an AJAX call (if applicable). When dealing with AJAX functionality, always be sure to comment on what each global APEX application variable (*x01–x10*) means.

Base Your Code Upon Templates

Having templates for plug-in code can really help speed up and standardize your coding process. By now you should realize that there are a lot of similarities among the different types of plug-in functions. You can create a generic template for all types of plug-in functions or more specific templates based on the plug-in and function type.

For JavaScript, using the jQuery UI Widget Factory definitely helps out. A template is provided in Chapter 8 that will work in just about any environment. You may also want to augment the template with additional commenting and code that supports your corporate standards.

Versioning External Files

Some web servers will instruct browsers to cache certain types of files. This helps reduce network load and speed up the time it takes for a page to load, since it does not need to wait for files to download.

Browser caching can present a small problem if your plug-in contains certain external files such as a JavaScript or CSS files. If you update a file for a plug-in, the browser may still use the old (cached) version until the file's expiration date. If your application relies on the newer version of the file, users will encounter an issue.

There are several ways to get around the browser caching issue, but one of the easiest ways is to simply rename the file each time you make a change. For example, if your plug-in contains a file called myPlugin.js, rename it to myPlugin.1.0.0.js. The next time you make a change to the file, rename the file again (in this example to myPlugin.1.0.1.js) and the browser will recognize it as a new file. The only catch with this technique is that you need to remember to modify your plug-in's render function and reference the new file name.

The following example demonstrates this problem and the impact of renaming a file. To keep things simple, the example does not use a plug-in, but the principles are essentially the same for a file that is loaded as part of a plug-in.

▬ **Note** The following set of instructions assumes that you have installed a local Apache web server. If you have not installed Apache, please refer to the installation instructions in Chapter 8 before continuing with this section.

This demo uses Google Chrome to leverage some of its network traffic display tools. If you do not have this browser installed, you can download and install it from http://www.google.com/chrome. The remaining part of this demo assumes that you are running it in Google Chrome.

Configure your Apache server.

a. It is common practice for web servers to explicitly tell the browser how long to cache a file. These next steps will modify the Apache server to set the default cache timeout (called *Expires*) in Apache.

b. In Windows, open Notepad in administrator mode. To run in administrator mode, right-click the application on the menu and select Run as administrator as shown in Figure 7-2 In earlier versions of Windows, you may not be required to use the Run as administrator feature.

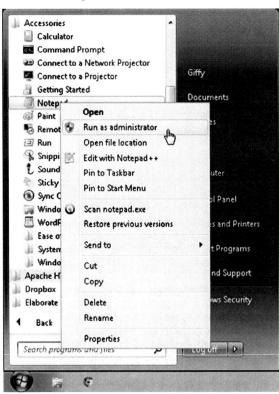

Figure 7-2. Open Notepad as administrator

    c.   In Notepad, open the Apache configuration file, `httpd.conf`, from the location defined in Chapter 8, Debugging & Tools. Figure 7-3 shows the default location on Windows 7.

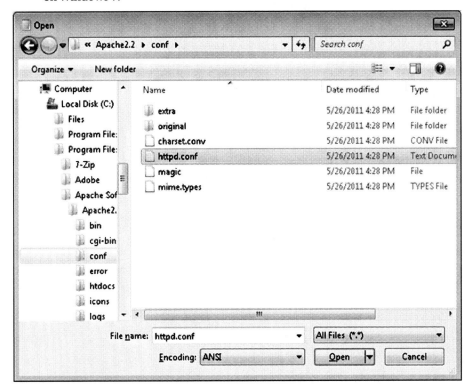

Figure 7-3. Open Apache `httpd.conf` file

    d.   Search the file for **expires**. The first result should bring you to the following line: `#LoadModuleexpires_module modules/mod_expires.so`. Uncomment this line by removing the hash (#) symbol.

    e.   Search the file for `<IfModulecgid_module>`. Just above this line, add the following lines:

```
<IfModule mod_expires.c>
     ExpiresActive on
     ExpiresByType text/javascript "access plus 60 seconds"
     ExpiresByType application/javascript "access plus 60 seconds"
</IfModule>
```

This setting will cache JavaScript files from your local web server for 60 seconds. Of course, web servers can cache files for a much longer period of time, but this is just for demo purposes.

f. Save the file and then restart the Apache server. To restart the Apache server, click Start   All Programs   Apache HTTP Server 2.2   Control Apache Server Restart as shown in Figure 7-4.

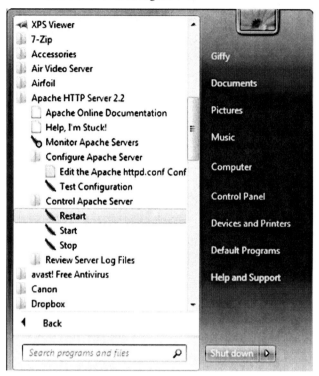

Figure 7-4. Restart Apache HTTP server

Set up the demo.

Create a new directory: c:\www\browserCachDemo.

Create a new file in c:\www\browserCachDemo called apressDemo.js.

Edit apressDemo.js by entering console.log('version 1'); and save your changes. You may want to leave this file open in your text editor, as you'll be modifying it later in this example.

Create a new blank page with the following settings:

Page Type: **Blank Page**
Page Number: **50**
Name: **Cache Demo**
Tab: **Cache Demo**

Edit Page 50. Right-click the Cache Demo link and select Edit from the content menu as shown in Figure 7-5.

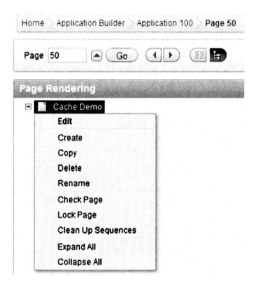

Figure 7-5. Edit Page 50

It the HTML Header and Body Attribute section, enter the following in the HTML Header text box as shown in Figure 7-6.

```
<script src="http://localhost/browserCachDemo/apressDemo.js"
type="text/javascript"></script>
```

Click the Apply changes button.

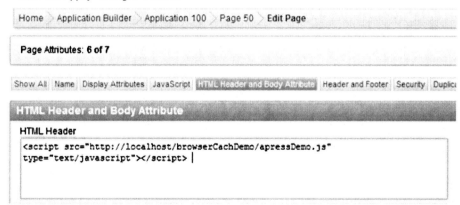

Figure 7-6. Page 50 HTML Header and Body Attribute tab

Create a new HTML region on Page 50 called Cache Demo.

Add a region button to the Cache Demo region with the following attributes:

> *Button Name:* **RELOAD_PAGE**
> *Position:* **Bottom of Region**
> *Alignment:* **Left**
> *Action:* **Redirect to Page in this Application**
> *Page:* **50**
>
> This button will be used to simulate someone clicking a link to the page. If you refresh the page using the browser's refresh button, it will automatically fetch the files from the web server rather than using cached versions.

View the initial browser request.

Go back to the main `Application 100` page in the `Application Builder`. Click the big `Run Application` button.

On the run page, you can log in to the application and continue to Page 50.

Open the JavaScript console by pressing Ctrl+Shift+J.

On the JavaScript console, click the `Network` tab and filter by clicking the `Scripts` button. Figure 7-7 highlights these two buttons.

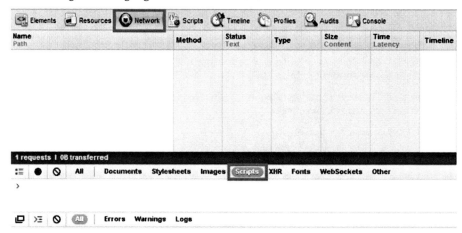

Figure 7-7. Google Chrome JavaScript console configuration

Click the `Cache Demo` tab at the top of the page. The JavaScript console should look like Figure 7-8. The two things to note from Figure 7-8 are that the `Status` for `apressDemo.js` is `200 OK` and that the console printed `version 1` as expected. `200 OK` means that it downloaded the file from the web server.

Figure 7-9 shows the network timeline for the file load. You'll notice that it took ~300ms to get the file from the server.

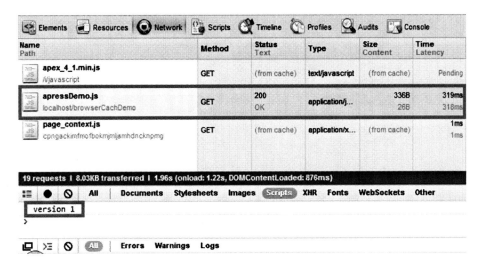

Figure 7-8. JavaScript console network information for initial file load

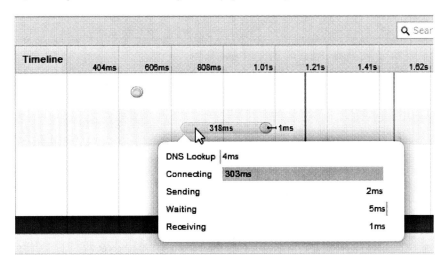

Figure 7-9. JavaScript console network timeline for initial file load

If you click the apressDemo.js file in Figure 7-8, you will see the header information for the file. The most important thing is the Expires attribute which is highlighted in Figure 7-10. Notice that it's exactly 60 seconds after the time in the Date field. This means that the browser should use the local copy for the next 60 seconds. After that, it should request a new copy from the server. As previously mentioned, the Expires tag is usually set for a much longer time frame.

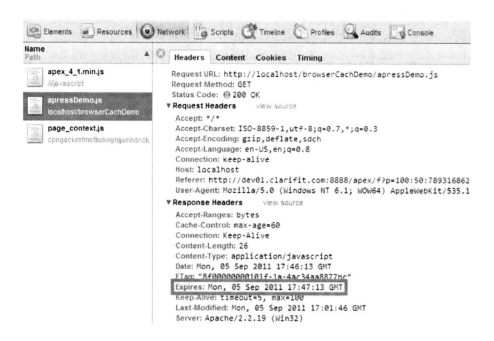

Figure 7-10. Network header information for apressDemo.js

Before reloading the page, update the JavaScript file (apressDemo.js) and change the text from version 1 to version 2.

Click the Reload Page button, which simulates a link on another page going to Page 50.

Figure 7-11 shows the network panel from the developer console. A few things stand out. This time apressDemo.js was retrieved from cache rather than from the web server (assuming that you reloaded the page within 60 seconds of the previous page view). This is explicitly stated in the Status column.

The other thing is that in the console area, it shows version 1, even though the JavaScript file was updated with the text version 2. This is expected, since apressDemo.js was loaded from cache rather than from the file server.

Figure 7-12 shows the timeline for this page request. You'll notice that it took no time to get the files since they were already in cache.

Figure 7-11. JavaScript console network information for page reload

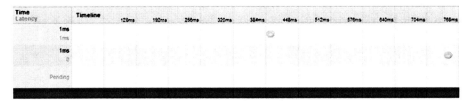

Figure 7-12. JavaScript console network timeline for page reload

You can now see that using a cached file can create some issues, since the client's browser may not be using the current version of a file on your web server. By no means is it a bad thing to have cached files (it's actually a very good thing), but you need to be aware of its impact on your plug-ins that use external files.

The way to get around this is pretty simple. If you use a unique file name for each change that is made to an external file, the browser will consider it as a new file and always retrieve it (at least once) from the server.

The easiest way to ensure a unique file name is to add a suffix to the filename with a version number and increase that version number for each change. The following steps demonstrate how to simply do this working from the previous example.

Make a copy of apressDemo.js and call it apressDemo2.js. By making a copy of the file, you ensure that any old apps that reference the old version still work.

Edit Page 50 (see Figure 7-8) and go to the HTML Header and Body Attribute section. Change the file name from apressDemo.js to apressDemo2.js as shown in Figure 7-13.

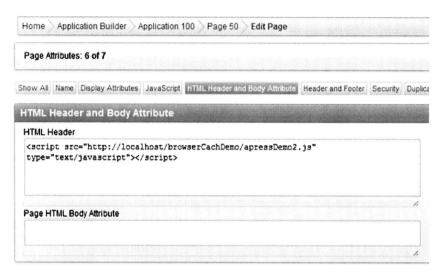

Figure 7-13. HTML Header and Body Attribute apressDemo2.js reference

Go back to the application and click the Reload Page button. The developer console
window should look like Figure 7-14

You can now see that the browser assumes apressDemo2.js is a new file and
retrieves it from the web server rather than its cache. The JavaScript console
also displays the correct message.

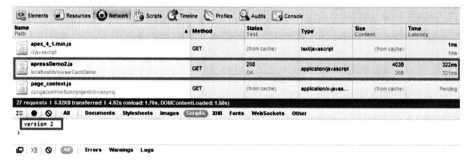

Figure 7-14. Developer console for apressDemo2.js

This section covered in detail the effects of browser caching external files and how to work around
this issue. It is extremely important that you remember and understand this, as it can help prevent
problems in the long run.

Compress JavaScript and CSS Files

To help reduce bandwidth and improve overall page load time, you should minimize your JavaScript and CSS files. Minimizing these files reduces the amount of text in the file to a bare minimum. Minimizing files makes the code unreadable by humans, so it's usually done as a last step before the plug-in is released.

There are several free minimization tools available to minimize JavaScript and CSS files. Wikipedia has a good list of these tools at http://en.wikipedia.org/wiki/Minification_(programming).

To give an example of how much space a minimized file can save compared to the full version, jquery.ui.clarifitFromToDatePicker_1.0.0.js was minimized using the YUI Compressor tool (http://developer.yahoo.com/yui/compressor/). The original file size was 5.36KB, whereas the compressed version is 2.06KB. For larger files, you'll see larger gains. Figure 7-15 shows part of the output of the minimized version.

```
1    (function(a){a.widget("ui.clarifitFromToDatePicker",{options:{
     correspondingDatePicker:{dateFormat:"",id:"",value:""},datePickerAttrs
     :{autoSize:true,buttonImage:"",buttonImageOnly:true,changeMonth:true,
     changeYear:true,dateFormat:"mm/dd/yy",showAnim:"",showOn:"button"},
     datePickerType:"",},_init:function(){var b=this;a.console.log(b._scope,
     "_init",b);},_setWidgetVars:function(){var b=this;b._scope=
     "ui.clarifitFromToDatePicker";b._values={shortYearCutoff:30,};b.
     _elements={$otherDate:null};},_create:function(){var f=this;f.
     _setWidgetVars();var g=f._scope+"_create";a.console.groupCollapsed(g);a
     .console.log("this:",f);a.console.log("element:",f.element[0]);var c=a(
     f.element),b,e="",h="";try{b=f.options.correspondingDatePicker.value!=
     ""?a.datepicker.parseDate(f.options.correspondingDatePicker.dateFormat,
     f.options.correspondingDatePicker.value,{shortYearCutoff:f._values.
     shortYearCutoff}):"";e=f.options.datePickerType=="to"?b:"",h=f.options.
     datePickerType=="from"?b:"";f._elements.$otherDate=a("="+f.options.
     correspondingDatePicker.id);}catch(d){a.console.warn("Invalid Other
     Date",f);}c.datepicker({autoSize:f.options.datePickerAttrs.autoSize,
     buttonImage:f.options.datePickerAttrs.buttonImage,buttonImageOnly:f.
     options.datePickerAttrs.buttonImageOnly,changeMonth:f.options.
     datePickerAttrs.changeMonth,changeYear:f.options.datePickerAttrs.
     changeYear,dateFormat:f.options.datePickerAttrs.dateFormat,minDate:e,
     maxDate:h,showAnim:f.options.datePickerAttrs.showAnim,showOn:f.options.
```

Figure 7-15. Part of minimized jquery.ui.clarifitFromToDatePicker_1.0.0.js

If your plug-in uses multiple JavaScript files, you can minimize all of them and merge them into one file. Though this makes one "large" file, it reduces the number of network requests to the server. Reducing the number of network requests usually speeds up page load time in your application (unless it's a very large file).

To make it easier for you to quickly review the files as a learning tool, the examples in this book did not contain minimized JavaScript and CSS files.

Put Thought Into Your Error Handling

Managing errors for plug-ins can be a tricky thing. The biggest question is, do you raise a hard error (i.e., completely stop everything) or do you raise a soft error and allow the user to continue using the application?

The answer is... "It depends." To help determine how to handle each type of error you expect to encounter, you need to put yourself in the user's shoes. Ask yourself this: "Can the user properly continue if this error occurs?"

For a simple example, think about an item plug-in. If you encounter an error in the render function (i.e., the function that displays the item), what should you do? At a high level you have two options: raise an application error, making the page unusable by the user, or try to soften the blow and display a generic Unhandled error occurred. Please contact your system administrator. error message. In this case, it would make sense to raise an application error; the user couldn't, and probably shouldn't, continue with the application, since it's missing some data that it expects the user to see and modify.

For an example of a soft error, imagine that an error occurs in an AJAX function on the server/PL/SQL side. If you raise an application error in the PL/SQL block, it really doesn't do much, as the user won't get the error message. Instead, they're left waiting for an expected response from the server. As a workaround, you can explicitly catch errors and then send a message back to the JavaScript code letting it know what has happened. The JavaScript code can then display a soft error message to the user. This technique is shown in Chapter [insert number], Region Plug-in.

Write Good Help Text

Plug-ins allow for help text in two main areas: the plug-in and custom attributes. Overall, plug-in help can be added by editing the plug-in and going to the Help Text section as shown in Figure 7-16. The plug-in help text is in HTML markup.

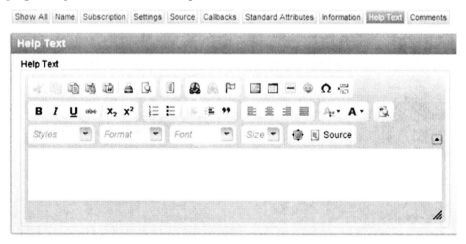

Figure 7-16. Plug-in help text

To add/modify help text for a custom attribute, edit the custom attribute and scroll to the Help Text region shown in Figure 7-17. The help text supports HTML markup (though you'll need to type it manually) and becomes available when a developer clicks the custom attribute label when using the plug-in as shown in Figure 7-18.

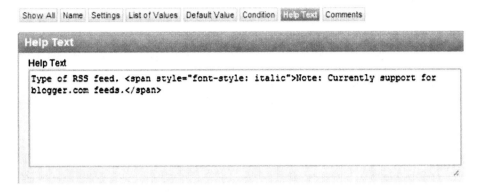

Figure 7-18. Custom attribute help text

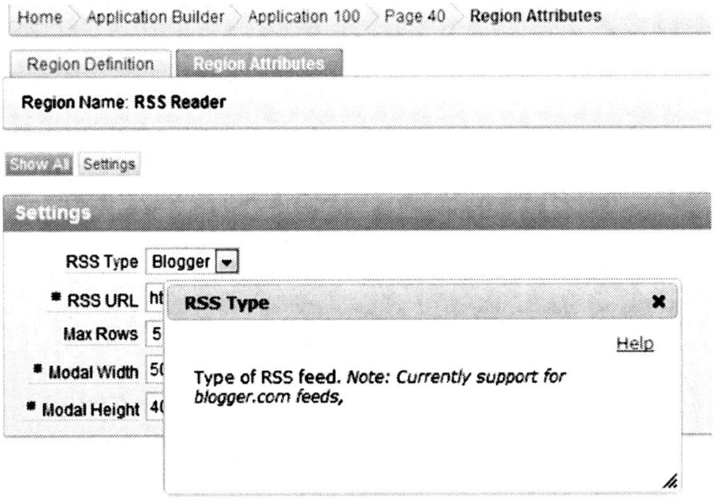

Figure 7-19. RSS Reader: RSS Type help text

Since plug-ins are used by other APEX developers, the help text should be written in language that is appropriate for other developers (i.e., end users won't be viewing this help text). The examples in this book did not contain help text since they were described in detail.

Participate in the Plug-in Community

The APEX community has really embraced plug-ins and has written a lot of excellent blog articles, as well as posting some free plug-ins online for other developers to use and learn from. The following is a list of some useful web sites and blogs:

> `http://apex-plugin.com`: Most developers will post their plug-ins on this site for others to use.

> `http://plugins.clarifit.com`: Plug-in demo site maintained by ClariFit.

> `http://skillbuilders.com/plugins`: Plug-in demo site maintained by Skillbuilders.

> `http://www.TalkApex.com`: Blog (by yours truly) with some posts on plug-in development.

> `http://www.danielmcghan.us`: Blog by Dan McGhan, who writes most of Skillbuilders plug-ins.

> `http://blog.theapexfreelancer.com`: Blog by Matt Nolan, who has created some commercial plug-ins.

> `http://www.inside-oracle-apex.com`: Blog by Patrick Wolf from Oracle. He created plug-ins for APEX.

> `http://apexblogs.info`: APEX blog RSS aggregator that has some plug in–specific content.

By far the best site to get APEX plug-ins is `http://apex-plugin.com/`. This site allows any APEX developer to post a plug-in for others to use. Most of these plug-ins are free, but some require a license. You are encouraged to go to the site and try some of the plug-ins. If you do create a plug-in for public consumption, you are encouraged to post it on this site.

The plug-ins on `apex-plugin.com` are not created or supported by Oracle, so you should be slightly cautious about using them in your applications. Though the APEX community is a small and trustworthy one, there is still a possibility that someone may post a plug-in with malicious code, or a plug-in may have a security vulnerability. The following blog posts discuss this issue in detail, with some excellent feedback from some of the experts in the field: `http://www.talkapex.com/2011/04/malicious-code-in-apex-plugins.html` and `http://www.talkapex.com/2011/04/malicious-code-in-apex-plugins-feedback.html`.

The articles also discuss scalability issues when using others' plug-ins. Though this is an area of concern, it must be taken with a grain of salt. If you only have a small set of users on your system, scalability may not be a concern. On the flip side, if you have thousands—or hundreds of thousands—of users, then scalability is a very big concern and you should modify the open-source plug-in to fit your needs and requirements.

Oracle also has some plug-ins which they maintain. To view this list, edit your application. Go to Shared Components ▸ Plug-ins. Click the `View Plug-in Repository` button as shown in Figure 7-19. This will open another web page, which will direct you to Oracle's plug-in repository.

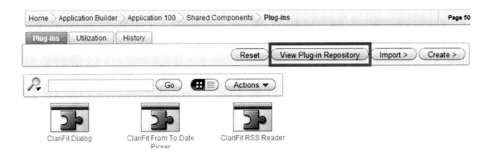

Figure 7-20. View Plug-in Repository

Summary

This chapter covered some of the best practices to follow when creating plug-ins. Again, these are recommendations, and you should modify and add to them to coincide with your organization's standards. The main thing to take away from these best practices is that you're aware of them and understand the consequences of using or not using them.

This chapter also covered how you can participate in the APEX plug-in community. There are a lot of benefits to participating in a plug-in community. Even if you can't publish your plug-ins, you can at least provide feedback and comments to enhance existing plug-ins.

CHAPTER 8

Debugging & Tools

Developing plug-ins, especially your first plug-in, can be difficult without the appropriate tools and debugging techniques. This chapter discusses how to instrument your plug-in. It also covers some tools to help assist and speed up your plug-in development.

Debugging and Code Instrumentation

Instrumenting your plug-ins will help quickly and effectively resolve issues as you encounter them. In some cases where your plug-in is used in other environments (i.e., you publish for others to use), you may not have the luxury of viewing the application and will need to solely rely on what information you can get from various debugging and logging tools.

This section will cover how to instrument both PL/SQL and JavaScript code. It is important to instrument both parts, as they can both play major roles in your plug-ins.

JavaScript Console Wrapper

When writing JavaScript code for a plug-in, it is important to add as much debugging code as possible. This can be extremely useful for debugging your own issues during the initial phases of plug-in development and for resolving them once they are in production or others are using them.

Before continuing with this section, you should read the section under Tools Firebug and Console in the Firefox on how to install and view Console outputs.

At a high level, Console allows you to add some additional code in JavaScript, which will display the results in a special window. This means that you do not need to interrupt the user with debugging messages, etc.

Some of the older browsers do not support JavaScript calls to the Console APIs. This can be a bit of an annoyance since you may instrument your code with `console.log` calls and then have to remove them before going to production.

APEX provides you with a simple JavaScript function called `apex.debug`. It handles the browser–specific issues so you can keep it in your code and it will not crash applications that are run in older browsers. When used, it will only display messages in the Console window when the application is run in debug mode.

Figure 8-1 shows a simple example of the `apex.debug` function when the application is run in regular (non-debug) mode. You'll notice that nothing was displayed in the Console window. Figure 8-2 shows the exact same call when the application is run in debug mode. In this case, a message was displayed in the Console window.

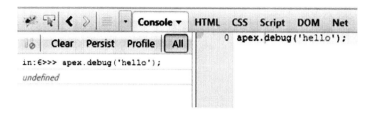

Figure 8-1. apex.debug in regular (non-debug) mode

Figure 8-2. apex.debug in debug mode

Apex.debug is good for basic messages, but it does not handle more complex logging requirements. Console Wrapper is a third–party, open–source library that handles both basic and complex logging requirements. It also is tightly integrated with APEX so that, by default, it only displays Console messages when the application is run in debug mode. All the JavaScript examples in this book leverage Console Wrapper, which can be downloaded for free at http://code.google.com/p/js-console-wrapper.

The web site provides detailed examples and information on how to use the Console Wrapper. The following are some examples of Console Wrapper compared with the apex.debug function. Note that these examples should be run directly in the Console window with your APEX application running in debug mode.

Figure 8-3 demonstrates how to reference multiple variables in one call. You'll notice that the apex.debug method only displays the first value. To get around this, you'd need to make an individual call for each variable with apex.debug. Console Wrapper handles unlimited variables in one call.

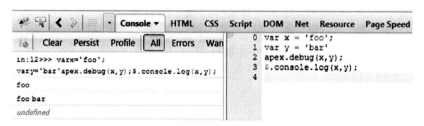

Figure 8-3. Console Wrapper: multiple values

Error! Reference source not found. Groups can be nested. If you want your group to be collapsed by default, use the $.console.groupCollapsed function instead of $.console.group.

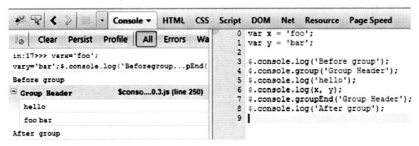

Figure 8-4. Console Wrapper: grouping

Console Wrapper also includes a very helpful function to display all the parameters in a function without having to explicitly list each parameter. Figure 8-5 shows how to use the $.console.logParams function. It also has additional checks in place to show parameters that are not explicitly linked to an input parameter. Figure 8-6 highlights this functionality.

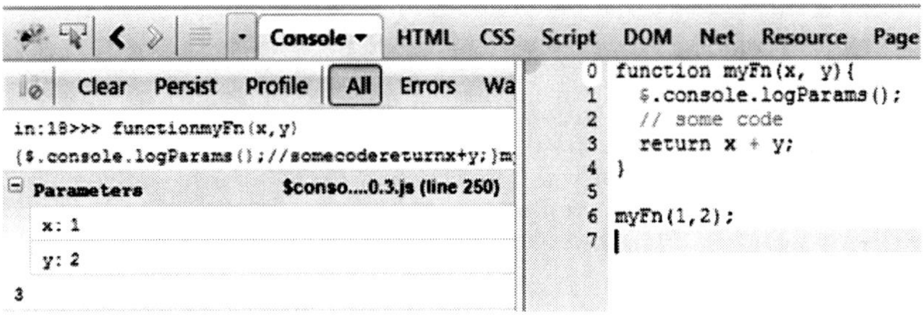

Figure 8-5. Console Wrapper: log parameters.

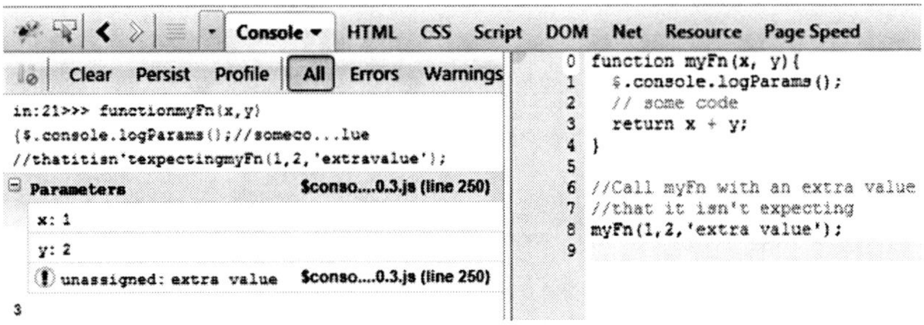

Figure 8-6. Console Wrapper: log parameters with unexpected parameters.

APEX Debug

Just like instrumenting your JavaScript code, it's equally important to instrument your PL/SQL plug-in code. APEX makes instrumenting plug-ins very simple by providing API debugging functions for each type of plug-in. All of the examples in this book leverage these API calls.

At the beginning of each plug-in, you should always reference the appropriate debug procedure based on the plug-in type. The procedure looks like `APEX_PLUGIN_UTIL.DEBUG_<plugin-type>`. For example, the region type debug procedure call is `APEX_PLUGIN_UTIL.DEBUG_REGION`. Additional information about each of these procedures can be found in the API documentation.

The following example shows how you can view the output from the plug-in debug call and what type of information it stores. This example references the region plug-in that was created in the chapter on region plug-ins.

1. Log into the APEX Application Builder, then run the demo application. Logging into the APEX Application Builder first allows you to easily run the application in debug mode.

2. Run the application and go to page 40 (RSS reader). At the bottom of the page, click the *Debug* button in the APEX Developer Toolbar as shown in Figure 8-7.

Figure 8-7. APEX Developer Toolbar

3. When you click the *Debug* button, the page reloads and it appears as though nothing happened. In fact, when the page reloaded, it stored a lot of debug information. To view this information, click the *View Debug* button (to the left of the *Debug* button) on the APEX Developer Toolbar as shown in Figure 8-7. A new window should pop up, which should look like Figure 8-8.

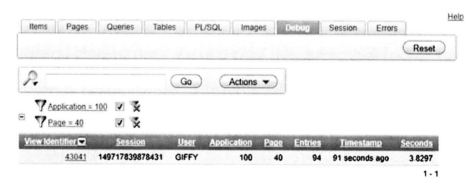

Figure 8-8. APEX debug message data window

4. Click on the most recent page–view link. From Figure 8-8, this would be *43041* under the *View Identifier* column. Since the *View Identifier* number is a unique number, it will probably be a different number.

5. Search the page for *Region: RSS Reader*. You'll notice that following this line, there is a lot of plug-in-specific information, as shown in Figure 8-9. If the plug-in had not made a call to `APEX_PLUGIN_UTIL.DEBUG_REGION`, this information would not be available in the debug window.

1.49307	0.10097	Region: RSS Reader	4	
1.59439	0.10793	...Execute Statement: begin declare begin wwv_flow_plugin.g_region_render_result := pkg_apress_plugins.f_render_rss_reader (p_region => wwv_flow_plugin.g_region,p_plugin => wwv_flow_plugin.g_plugin,p_is_printer_friendly => (:p_is_printer_friendly='Y'));end; end;	4	
1.70196	0.00863	Plugin meta data:	4	
1.71076	0.01133	file_prefix: http://localhost/RSSReader/	4	
1.72188	0.00622	attribute_01:	4	
1.72813	0.00701	attribute_02:	4	
1.73516	0.01040	attribute_03:	4	
1.74573	0.00689	attribute_04:	4	
1.75251	0.00704	attribute_05:	4	
1.75955	0.00669	attribute_06:	4	
1.76614	0.00589	attribute_07:	4	
1.77203	0.00615	attribute_08:	4	
1.77819	0.00565	attribute_09:	4	
1.78413	0.00855	attribute_10:	4	
1.79247	0.00680	attribute_11:	4	
1.79923	0.00633	attribute_12:	4	
1.80558	0.00582	attribute_13:	4	
1.81144	0.00840	attribute_14:	4	
1.81976	0.00507	attribute_15:	4	
1.82502	0.00582	Region meta data:	4	
1.83073	0.00794	id: 3668601226427952	4	
1.83963	0.00937	static_id: R3668601226427952	4	
1.84795	0.00572	name: RSS Reader	4	
1.85393	0.00813	type: PLUGIN_COM.CLARIFIT.APEXPLUGIN.RSS_READER	4	
1.86217	0.00788	source:	4	
1.86984	0.00668	ajax_items_to_submit:	4	
1.87690	0.00933	escape_output: false	4	
1.88590	0.00836	attribute_01: blogger	4	
1.89414	0.00671	attribute_02: http://www.talkapex.com/feeds/posts/default	4	
1.90109	0.00837	attribute_03: 5	4	
1.90941	0.00755	attribute_04: 500	4	
1.91674	0.00506	attribute_05: 400	4	
1.92188	0.00598	attribute_06:	4	

Figure 8-9. Plug-in debug output

You can include additional debug messages throughout your plug-in by using the `APEX_DEBUG_MESSAGE` API calls. These messages will appear in the same debug report as Figure 8-9. Please read the API documentation for more information about this package.

Tools

When coding, developers tend to have a set of tools to help speed up their development time. This section will cover some tools that can be helpful when developing plug-ins. They are used and mentioned throughout the book so you should take the time to review and understand each one.

Firebug and Console in the Firefox Browser

Firefox is an excellent browser to develop web–based applications with (some developers deem it as the best browser for development). It has a lot of great features and available add-ons that help developers.

Firebug is a very popular Firefox add-on that allows you to, among other things, debug and quickly develop/test JavaScript code. I often use Firebug as my default development and debugging tool. In some situations, though, I leverage Google Chrome's development tools for their debugging features. Both browsers support the Console API, which allows you to display messages in the browser's Console window without interrupting the user. The following steps cover how to install Firebug on Firefox 4.

▨ **Note** Console is also available in most of the major browsers. The following list describes how to view the Console output in each of the major browsers:

- Firefox: Install Firebug (http://getfirebug.com) - F12
- Google Chrome: Ctrl+Shift+J
- Safari: Ctrl+Alt+C
- IE (9+): F12, then go to the Console tab

---

1. Make sure that you've installed Firefox 4 or greater. If you haven't, you can download it at http://www.mozilla.com.

6. In the top–left corner, click the *Firefox* button and select the *Add-ons* menu option, as shown in Figure 8-10, which will open a new tab. Alternatively, you can use the shortcut *Ctrl+Shift+A*.

Figure 8-10. Firefox Add-ons

7. On the *Add-ons Manage* tab, enter **firebug** in the search field in the top–right corner and click *enter* to submit your search.

8. Click the *Install* button beside the Firebug search result (third option in Figure 8-11).

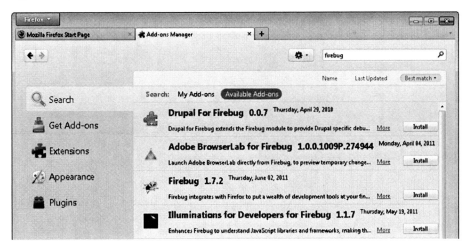

Figure 8-11. Install Firebug

9. Once installed, you'll need to restart Firefox for Firebug to be activated.

Now that Firebug is installed, you'll need to configure it to enable the Console. The Console allows you to quickly output debug messages and view errors and warnings in JavaScript. The following steps enable the Console:

1. In Firefox, go to any web site and click the F12 button. The Firebug window will appear at the bottom of the screen. Click on the *Console* tab and select *Enabled* under its menu as shown in Figure 8-12.

Figure 8-12. Enable Firebug Console.

2. The Console window should now appear on the screen. The last thing you need to do is display the command window, which will allow you to run your own JavaScript code. Click the *Console* tab and check *Command Editor* as shown in Figure 8-13.

Figure 8-13. Enable Console Command Editor

3. The Firebug screen should now display the Command Editor window as shown in Figure 8-14.

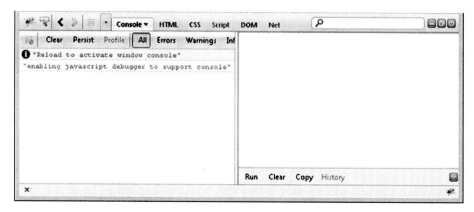

Figure 8-14. Console Command Editor

From the Console Command Editor, you can run any JavaScript commands to test your code. It usually helps to develop the code in the editor first, then move it into a static file. The advantage of this approach is that you don't need to refresh your page each time you make a modification.

Console also provides a great logging API. The following links contain examples and screenshots of the logging API:

- http://getfirebug.com/logging - Intro and screenshots

- http://www.tuttoaster.com/learning-javascript-and-dom-with-console - Step-by-step demos and screenshots

- http://getfirebug.com/wiki/index.php/Console_API - Console API

jQuery UI Widget Factory

When developing certain types of plug-ins, you will need to include some custom JavaScript code. In some cases, this JavaScript code will be fairly simple. In other cases, the code may be more complex. When developing more complex code, it helps to use a framework to standardize and simplify some of the process.

The jQuery UI Widget Factory is a framework that allows you to build custom JavaScript code. It is an extension of jQuery UI, which is already included with APEX, so there is no additional code that you need to add in order to leverage your plug-ins.

This section will cover some of the basic structure around building code that leverages the Widget Factory. It does not include all the information about the framework, but rather a brief summary to help you get started. For more information, please read the main documentation page: http://docs.jquery.com/UI_Developer_Guide#The_widget_factory.

The example below is a simple widget built using the jQuery UI Widget Factory framework that will toggle the font size of an element. It is very basic and perfect for highlighting the fundamental items that are required for the Widget Factory. It also includes some logging code to help highlight the functions when called. The logging code uses the Console Wrapper library (http://code.google.com/p/js-console-wrapper/).

▓ **Note** Special thanks to Dan McGhan for helping come up with some of the standards when using the jQuery UI Widget Factory.

```
$.widget('ui.toggleFontSize', {
  // default options
  options: {
    toggleFontSize: '40px' // Default the toggle font to bold if one not provided
  },

  /**
   * Set private widget varables
   */
  _setWidgetVars: function(){
    var uiw = this;

    uiw._scope = 'ui.toggleFontSize'; //For debugging

    uiw._values = {
      baseFontSize: '', // This is the font size that the text started with.
    };

    uiw._elements = {
      $element : $(uiw.element) //Enter elements here for quick reference
    };
  }, //_setWidgetVars

  /**
   * Create function: Called the first time widget is associated to the object
   * Will implicitly call the _init function after
   */
  _create: function(){
    var uiw = this;

    uiw._setWidgetVars(); // Set variables

    var consoleGroupName = uiw._scope + '_create';
    $.console.groupCollapsed(consoleGroupName);
    $.console.log('this:', uiw);

    uiw._values.baseFontSize = uiw._elements.$element.css('fontSize');

    $.console.groupEnd(consoleGroupName);
  },//_create
```

```
/**
 * Init function: This function will be called each time the widget is referenced with no
parameters.
 */
_init: function(){
  var uiw = this;

  $.console.log(uiw._scope, '_init', uiw);

  //Toggle Font Size
  if (uiw._elements.$element.css('fontSize') == uiw._values.baseFontSize){
    uiw._elements.$element.css('fontSize', uiw.options.toggleFontSize);
  }
  else{
    uiw._elements.$element.css('fontSize', uiw._values.baseFontSize);
  }
}, //_init

/**
 * Returns the base font size that the  object started with
 * Need to write a specific function since it's a private variable
 */
getBaseFontSize: function(){
  var uiw = this;

  $.console.log(uiw._scope, 'getBaseFontSize', uiw);
  return uiw._values.baseFontSize;
},//getBaseFontSize

/**
 * Removes all functionality associated with widget
 * In most cases in APEX, this won't be necessary
 */
destroy: function() {
  var uiw = this;
  $.console.log(uiw._scope, 'destroy', uiw);

  //restore the font size back to its original size
  uiw._elements.$element.css('fontSize', uiw._values.baseFontSize);

  $.Widget.prototype.destroy.apply(uiw, arguments); // default destroy
}//destroy

}); //ui.toggleFontSize
```

Here is the breakdown of each of the main elements from the preceding code:

$.widget(name, options): This line defines the widget. The name is a string,
which should be "*ui.xyz*" where *xyz* is the camel case name of your widget. The
options variable is a JSON object that contains both private and public variables
and functions.

_setWidgetVars: This function is used to define and set private variables. This is not a reserved function name in the jQuery UI Widget Factory, but rather a technique to store private variables.

options: *options* is a reserved name that consists of a set of public variables. The values that are placed in this variable are the default values. When the widget is called, the calling function can define each of these option values.

_create: The *_create* function is a reserved function that is run the first time the widget is bound to an object.

_init: The *_init* function is a reserved function that is called after the *_create* function and each time the widget is called with no parameters. The *_init* method is not required, and you may not require it for your APEX plug-ins.

getBaseFontSize: This is a custom function that is publicly accessible. It is required since the variable *baseFontSize* is a private variable and needs a specific getter method to retrieve its value.

destroy: The *destroy* method disassociates the widget from the object and should undo anything that the widget did to the object. In this example, the *destroy* method returns the font size back to its original state. The *destroy* method is not required and you probably won't need to implement it for APEX plug-ins.

To demonstrate how to use this widget, open ch08\jqueryUIWidgetFactory-Demo.html in Firefox. This file is included as part of the book's attached files. Once you have opened the file in Firefox, click F12 to open Firebug. This will allow you to see the log outputs in the Console window. Click each link in the order described below. Screenshots are included to highlight all the changes. Figure 8-15 shows the original state of the page.

foo

bar

Run this in Firefox with Firebug installed and console running (F12) and follow along with chapter 8.

1. $('#bar').toggleFontSize();
2. $('#bar').toggleFontSize();
3. $('#bar').toggleFontSize('option', 'toggleFontSize'); *Getter*
4. $('#bar').toggleFontSize('option', 'toggleFontSize','200px'); *Setter*
5. $('#bar').toggleFontSize();
6. $('#bar').toggleFontSize('destroy');
7. $('#bar').toggleFontSize({toggleFontSize: '80px'});
8. $('#bar').toggleFontSize('getBaseFontSize');

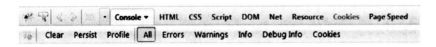

Figure 8-15. jQuery UI Widget Factory demo: initial page

1. `$('#bar').toggleFontSize()`: This will attach the widget to the object and toggle the font size to the default 40px since no option was passed in as shown in Figure 8-16. Notice how both the _create and _init functions were called.

foo

Run this in Firefox with Firebug installed and console running (F12) and follow along with chapter 8.

1. $('#bar').toggleFontSize();
2. $('#bar').toggleFontSize();
3. $('#bar').toggleFontSize('option', 'toggleFontSize'); *Getter*
4. $('#bar').toggleFontSize('option', 'toggleFontSize', '200px'); *Setter*
5. $('#bar').toggleFontSize();
6. $('#bar').toggleFontSize('destroy');
7. $('#bar').toggleFontSize({toggleFontSize: '80px'});
8. $('#bar').toggleFontSize('getBaseFontSize');

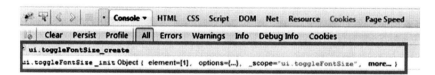

Figure 8-16. jQuery UI Widget Factory demo: step 1

10. `$('#bar').toggleFontSize()`: Will toggle the font back to its original size. It only calls the *_init* function since the widget has already been attached to the object. This can be seen in the Console window in Figure 8-17.

Run this in Firefox with Firebug installed and console running (F12) and follow along with chapter 8.

1. $('#bar').toggleFontSize();
2. $('#bar').toggleFontSize();
3. $('#bar').toggleFontSize('option', 'toggleFontSize'); *Getter*
4. $('#bar').toggleFontSize('option', 'toggleFontSize','200px'); *Setter*
5. $('#bar').toggleFontSize();
6. $('#bar').toggleFontSize('destroy');
7. $('#bar').toggleFontSize({toggleFontSize: '80px'});
8. $('#bar').toggleFontSize('getBaseFontSize');

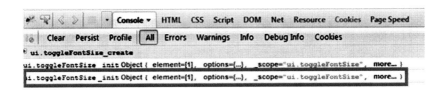

Figure 8-17. jQuery UI Widget Factory demo: step 2

11. `$('#bar').toggleFontSize('option', 'toggleFontSize')`: This is a getter method that can return any of the variables in the JSON *options* object. Since you haven't set the font size yet, this will return the default size, *40px*, as shown in Figure 8-18.

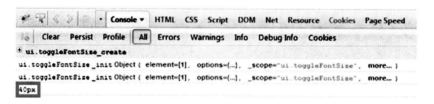

Figure 8-18. jQuery UI Widget Factory demo: step 3

12. `$('#bar').toggleFontSize('option', 'toggleFontSize','200px')`: This is a setter method that can set any of the items in the *options* object. It will return the jQuery object which is the *bar* item. It does not affect how *bar* is currently displayed on the page until it is toggled again.

13. `$('#bar').toggleFontSize()`: This will toggle the font size. Figure 8-19 shows that *bar* is much larger now. This is because it was set to 200px in the previous step.

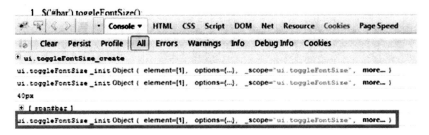

Figure 8-19. jQuery UI Widget Factory demo: step 5

14. `$('#bar').toggleFontSize('destroy')`: The destroy method removes the widget from the object and should undo anything that the widget did. Figure 8-20 shows that *bar* has been reset to its original state.

Run this in Firefox with Firebug installed and console running (F12) and follow along with chapter 8.

1. $('#bar').toggleFontSize();
2. $('#bar').toggleFontSize();
3. $('#bar').toggleFontSize('option', 'toggleFontSize'); *Getter*
4. $('#bar').toggleFontSize('option', 'toggleFontSize','200px'); *Setter*
5. $('#bar').toggleFontSize();
6. $('#bar').toggleFontSize('destroy');
7. $('#bar').toggleFontSize({toggleFontSize: '80px'});
8. $('#bar').toggleFontSize('getBaseFontSize');

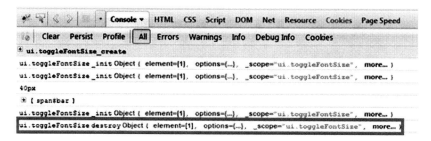

Figure 8-20. jQuery UI Widget Factory demo: step 6

15. `$('#bar').toggleFontSize({toggleFontSize: '80px'})`: This will attach the widget to the object. Since the widget was removed from the object in the previous step, both the *_create* and *_init* functions are executed as shown in Figure 8-21. This call is different than the first call in step 1 since it defines a value in the *option* object.

foo

Run this in Firefox with Firebug installed and console running (F12) and follow along with chapter 8.

1. $('#bar').toggleFontSize();
2. $('#bar').toggleFontSize();
3. $('#bar').toggleFontSize('option', 'toggleFontSize'); *Getter*
4. $('#bar').toggleFontSize('option', 'toggleFontSize', '200px'); *Setter*
5. $('#bar').toggleFontSize();
6. $('#bar').toggleFontSize('destroy');
7. $('#bar').toggleFontSize({toggleFontSize: '80px'});
8. $('#bar').toggleFontSize('getBaseFontSize');

```
Console ▼   HTML  CSS  Script  DOM  Net  Resource  Cookies  Page Speed

Clear  Persist  Profile  [All]  Errors  Warnings  Info  Debug Info  Cookies

⊕ ui.toggleFontSize_create
ui.toggleFontSize_init Object { element=[1], options={...}, _scope="ui.toggleFontSize", more... }
ui.toggleFontSize_init Object { element=[1], options={...}, _scope="ui.toggleFontSize", more... }
40px
⊕ [ span#bar ]
ui.toggleFontSize_init Object { element=[1], options={...}, _scope="ui.toggleFontSize", more... }
ui.toggleFontSize destroy Object { element=[1], options={...}, _scope="ui.toggleFontSize", more... }
ui.toggleFontSize_create
ui.toggleFontSize_init Object { element=[1], options={...}, _scope="ui.toggleFontSize", more... }
```

Figure 8-21. *jQuery UI Widget Factory demo: step 7*

16. `$('#bar').toggleFontSize('getBaseFontSize')`: To call a public function using the widget framework, pass in the function name. In this case, the function *getBaseFontSize* will return the private variable value *baseFontSize*, which is shown in Figure 8-22.

17. The final output of the Console window should look like Figure 8-22.

Figure 8-22. jQuery UI Widget Factory demo: final Console output

This section covered the basics of the jQuery UI Widget Factory framework and provided a simple example of how to create a widget. For plug-ins that require a very small amount of JavaScript, creating a widget may not be necessary. For more complex plug-ins, using the Widget Factory framework will help a lot.

Apache HTTP Server

Some of your plug-ins will require third–party files such as JavaScript, CSS, and images. When working with these files, it is highly recommended that you modify them directly from a web server before bundling them as part of the plug-in. In some situations, you may not have easy access to your corporate development web server or one may not exist. If this is the case, you can easily install a local web server on your desktop.

Apache HTTP Server is a free, open–source web server that is used in many corporate environments. The following instructions describe how to install and configure the Apache HTTP Server on Windows 7:

1. Go to `http://httpd.apache.org`. On the left–hand side, click *from a mirror* under the *Download* heading.

2. On the Download page, select the most recent stable build and download the Windows binary file as shown in Figure 8-23.

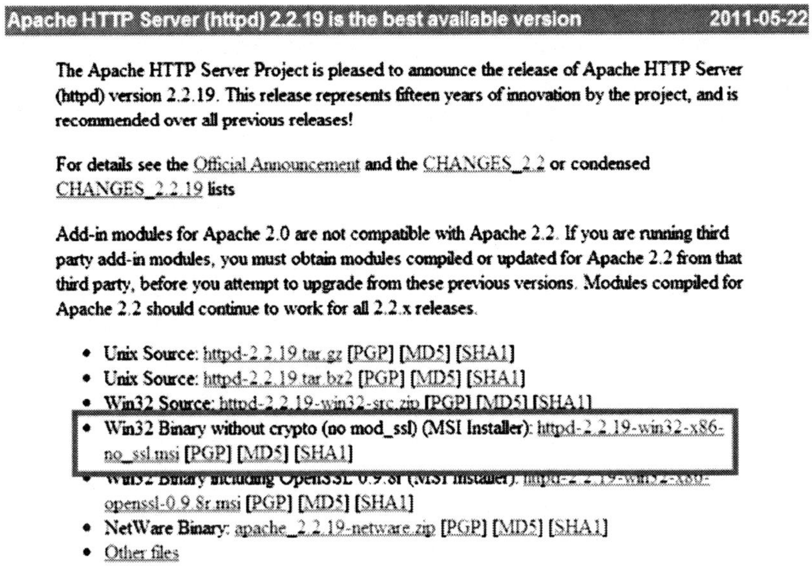

Apache HTTP Server (httpd) 2.2.19 is the best available version   **2011-05-22**

The Apache HTTP Server Project is pleased to announce the release of Apache HTTP Server (httpd) version 2.2.19. This release represents fifteen years of innovation by the project, and is recommended over all previous releases!

For details see the Official Announcement and the CHANGES_2.2 or condensed CHANGES_2.2.19 lists

Add-in modules for Apache 2.0 are not compatible with Apache 2.2. If you are running third party add-in modules, you must obtain modules compiled or updated for Apache 2.2 from that third party, before you attempt to upgrade from these previous versions. Modules compiled for Apache 2.2 should continue to work for all 2.2.x releases.

- Unix Source: httpd-2.2.19.tar.gz [PGP] [MD5] [SHA1]
- Unix Source: httpd-2.2.19.tar.bz2 [PGP] [MD5] [SHA1]
- Win32 Source: httpd-2.2.19-win32-src.zip [PGP] [MD5] [SHA1]
- Win32 Binary without crypto (no mod_ssl) (MSI Installer): httpd-2.2.19-win32-x86-no_ssl.msi [PGP] [MD5] [SHA1]
- Win32 Binary including OpenSSL 0.9.8r (MSI Installer): httpd-2.2.19-win32-x86-openssl-0.9.8r.msi [PGP] [MD5] [SHA1]
- NetWare Binary: apache_2.2.19-netware.zip [PGP] [MD5] [SHA1]
- Other files

Figure 8-23. Download Apache HTTP Server

3. Run the file once it has finished downloading. Keep clicking the *Next* button, reading the license agreement when prompted, until you come to the *Server Information* step. Since this will only be used for your personal development, you can enter any information here. Some example setup data is shown in Figure 8-24. Click the *Next* button to continue.

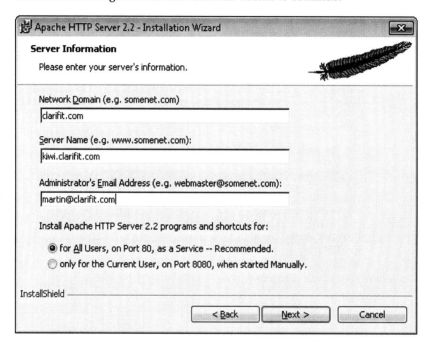

Figure 8-24. Apache HTTP Server information

4. Select *Typical* from the Setup Type window as shown in Figure 8-25. Click *Next* to continue.

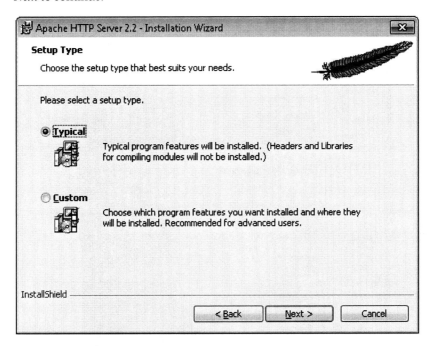

Figure 8-25. Apache HTTP setup type

5. On the next screen, *Destination Folder*, select the default location. Keep note of where this is on your computer, as you'll need it to find the configuration file. Click the *Next* button to proceed to the final step.

6. On the final screen, click *Install* to install the Apache HTTP Server. Once completed, click the *Finish* button.

After installing Apache, you'll need to configure it. The following steps describe how to configure the Apache Server for simple local use:

▨ **Note** In Windows 7, administrative privileges are required to edit the Apache configuration file. The instructions below include the additional steps required to modify the file as an administrator. If using an older version of Windows, you should be able to edit the file directly.

---

1. In Windows, click *Start All Programs Apache HTTP Server 2.2 Configure Apache Server*. Right click on *Edit the Apache httpd.conf Configuration File* and select *Open file location* as shown in Figure 8-26.

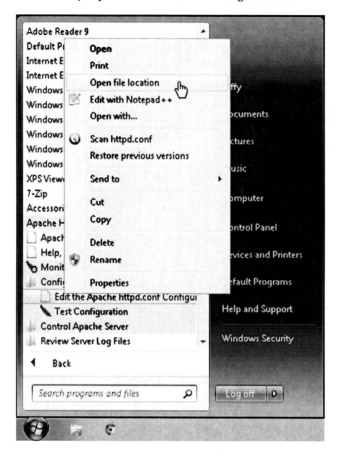

Figure 8-26. Open Apache config location

18. Copy or note the location of the file. In this example, the configuration file is located in `C:\Program Files (x86)\Apache Software Foundation\Apache2.2\conf` as shown in Figure 8-27.

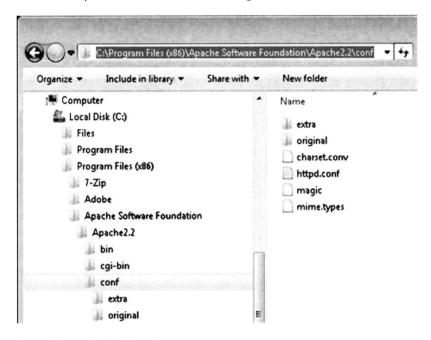

Figure 8-27. Apache configuration file location

19. Open *Notepad* as an administrator. Click *Start   All Programs   Accessories*. Right click on *Notepad* and select *Run as administrator* as show in Figure 8-28.

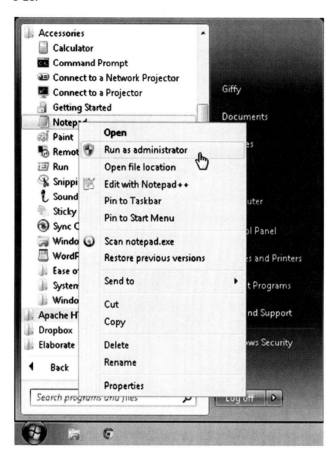

Figure 8-28. Open Notepad as administrator.

20. In Notepad, open the Apache configuration file, *httpd.conf*, from the location that was copied in step 2 as shown in Figure 8-29. You will need to change the file type to *All Files* in order to see *httpd.conf*.

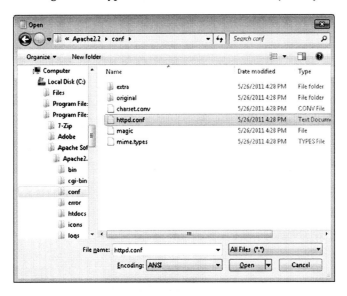

Figure 8-29. Open Apache httpd.conf file

21. The options that you will modify are to tell Apache where to look for the web files. There are two options that need to be changed to do this. The first is the *DocumentRoot*. Change the *DocumentRoot* from

```
DocumentRoot "C:/Program Files (x86)/Apache Software
Foundation/Apache2.2/htdocs"
```

to

DocumentRoot "C:/ www"

where c:/www points to a directory on your local machine. Apache is case–sensitive, so ensure that the *DocumentRoot* directory option has the same case as the directory on your file system. Apache also uses forward slashes (/) instead of back slashes (\) when referencing directories. Please note that the original *DocumentRoot* value may be different depending on you installation options.

203

22. When you modify the *DocumentRoot,* you also need to modify the corresponding *Directory* settings. Change the *Directory* option from

```
<Directory "C:/Program Files (x86)/Apache Software
Foundation/Apache2.2/htdocs">
```

to

`<Directory "C:/www">`

where `c:/www` is the same value from the *DocumentRoot* that you configured in the previous step.

23. Once you have modified the values, save the configuration file. If you haven't already done so, create the directory that you referenced in the configuration file.

24. The last step for the configuration is to restart the Apache HTTP Server. To restart it, click *Start All Programs Apache HTTP Server 2.2 Control Apache Server* and select *Restart.*

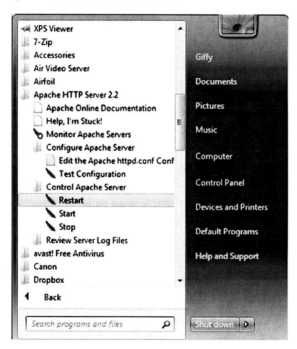

Figure 8-30. Restart Apache HTTP Server.

You can quickly test that your configuration works by creating a simple .html file in your *DocumentRoot* directory (in this case, `c:\www`). Then open your web browser and go to `http://localhost/mytestfile.html`.

APEX Dictionary and APIs

APEX comes with some excellent tools that can really help resolve some of your issues and speed up development. The APEX dictionary is one such tool. Each of the included APIs can be considered as a tool, too.

APEX Dictionary

Since APEX resides in the database, you can easily obtain all its information from querying certain views. Using these views can help you obtain additional information about specific objects in your APEX application.

APEX provides a view called the *APEX_DICTIONARY*, which lists all the views and their columns. The following query lists all the available views in the APEX dictionary. Figure 8-31 shows part of the result from the query below.

```
SELECT apex_view_name, comments
FROM apex_dictionary
WHERE column_id = 0
```

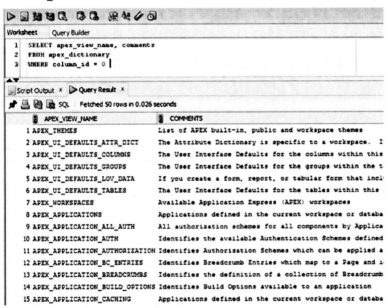

Figure 8-31. APEX Dictionary results

Some of these views were used in the plug-ins in this book to help retrieve additional information that was not available via the plug-in parameters. For example, in the from/to item–date picker, a view could be configured (*APEX_APPLICATION_PAGE_ITEMS*) to find some metadata about the *other* date item.

Below is a list of some of the APEX views that you will find very helpful when creating plug-ins:

Item plug-ins:`APEX_APPLICATION_ITEMS`

Dynamic action plug-ins:`APEX_APPLICATION_PAGE_DA` and `APEX_APPLICATION_PAGE_DA_ACTS`

Region plug-ins:`APEX_APPLICATION_PAGE_REGIONS`

Process plug-ins:`APEX_APPLICATION_PAGE_PROC` and `APEX_APPLICATION_PROCESSES`

The APEX dictionary is a very powerful tool that tends to get overlooked. You are encouraged to spend some time reviewing the views that are available.

APEX APIs

APEX provides a set of APIs that can help with your plug-in development. Examples of some of these APIs are used throughout this book. Here is a list of some of the most useful ones for plug-in development:

`APEX_CSS:` Handles CSS–related code

`APEX_JAVASCRIPT:` Handles JavaScript and JSON code. Good for escaping values in JavaScript as well.

`APEX_PLUGIN:` Primarily used for plug-in data types. Also contains a few functions to help with AJAX calls and item plug-ins.

`APEX_PLUGIN_UTIL:` Debugs calls for all types of plug-ins, along with some utility functions and procedures.

`JavaScript APIs:` JavaScript functions. Before writing your own functions to do something that you think should be part of APEX, look through this list.

Of course, you may use other packages not listed above. For a complete list of APIs, along with help and examples, view the APEX documentation. To get the latest copy of the APEX documentation, go to `http://apex.oracle.com` and click the *Application Express Documentation* under the *Getting Started* heading.

Summary

Spending time to instrument your code may initially seem like additional work. In the end, it always pays off to have this in your code. If you don't use it, another developer who has to work with it will.

There are a lot of tools you can use to help speed up development time. This chapter covers some of the most popular tools used by plug-in developers. There are other tools you may want to add to your repertoire that will help you with your development.

Again, it is worthwhile to spend the time up front and install/configure these tools. Once you have these tools in place, you will notice huge improvements on your development time.

INDEX

■ ■ ■

P, Q

CPSIA information can be obtained at www.ICGtesting.com
Printed in the USA
LVOW110144121211

258958LV00003B/189/P